# THE SPY
# BESIDE
# THE SEA

# THE SPY
# BESIDE
# THE SEA

## THE EXTRAORDINARY
## WARTIME STORY OF
## DOROTHY O'GRADY

ADRIAN SEARLE

*Front cover image*: *top*: map of the Isle of Wight. (Author's collection); *bottom*: prisoner 7250, Dorothy O'Grady, aged 20 – her initial prison photographs, taken at HMP Holloway in 1918. (The National Archives)

First published 2012

The History Press
The Mill, Brimscombe Port
Stroud, Gloucestershire, GL5 2QG
www.thehistorypress.co.uk

British Library Cataloguing in Publication Data.
A catalogue record for this book is available from the British Library.

ISBN 978 0 7524 7963 7

Typesetting and origination by The History Press
Printed in Great Britain

# CONTENTS

# ACKNOWLEDGEMENTS

Many people have contributed their time, guidance and professional expertise to aid the process – challenging and rewarding in equal measure – of unravelling the complexities underpinning what I believe to be the definitive story of Dorothy O'Grady. Without their invaluable input and support this book would not have been possible. Indeed, at one point, when key documentation was reportedly 'mislaid' at The National Archives, and remains to this day unavailable for inspection, the encouragement of family and friends was the principal factor which dissuaded me from 'throwing in the towel' after a protracted period of research.

I acknowledge particularly the support of my son and daughter-in-law, Matt and Sarah, both of whom have contributed significantly to illustrating 'the Dorothy book', researching O'Grady's familial background and checking the manuscript (along with other members of my family and my good friend, Jack Richards). I am also especially grateful to those with personal memories of Dorothy who have so willingly helped to illuminate the true character of this fascinating yet truly enigmatic woman. Their contributions are individually acknowledged in the text.

Many hours have been spent in an exhaustive examination, and re-examination, of archived material. The helpfulness and guidance of various professional custodians has substantially facilitated and enhanced the process. In this regard my thanks are extended in particular to staff at The National Archives in Kew, the British Library's newspaper library at Colindale, the Imperial War Museum's photographic collection, and the county records offices in the Isle of Wight and Essex. I am also grateful for the help of friends and former colleagues on the staffs of various newspapers who have searched their files for information and pictures.

The support and enthusiasm shown for this writing assignment from so many of my fellow Isle of Wight residents was important and is gratefully acknowledged. The O'Grady story has an obvious and particular resonance on the island, where it has long been enshrined in wartime folklore, awaiting final clarification of the truth behind it which this book project has sought to provide.

Finally, my thanks go to Mark Beynon (editor) and colleagues in the editorial and design teams at The History Press for entrusting me with this work and for the excellent job they collectively have made in guiding the production of the book.

# INTRODUCTION

Dorothy O'Grady has rightly been called the oddest spy of the Second World War. The 42-year-old landlady of a guest house beside the sea on the Isle of Wight, short in stature, plump, bespectacled and married to a retired fireman, she was – to put it mildly – very far removed from the archetypal 'cloak and dagger' image of an embedded enemy agent. She did not seem a woman committed to the cause of bringing the country in which she had always lived to its knees in the traumatic English summer of 1940.

But spies, in truth, come in all shapes, sizes and disguises. Against the backdrop of a nervous nation, fearing invasion and obsessed with spy scares (ignited to a large extent by irrational suspicion), the outwardly unremarkable Mrs O'Grady was summoned to a local courtroom in August for breaching the wartime Defence Regulations. There was nothing especially sensational about it. She had simply been found with her dog on the foreshore, in an area to which public access had been denied in the interests of national security, and where, of course, her presence posed a potential risk to the operations of soldiers charged with keeping the enemy at the door from crossing the British threshold.

Yet, this was the start of a truly remarkable, barely believable, chronicle of events destined to grab worldwide attention as one of the most compelling 'home front' mysteries of the war. It is a story that, for the want of one crucial element, has provoked discussion, argument, bewilderment and controversy ever since.

Until now, Dorothy O'Grady's story has been open to interpretation, and has indeed been interpreted several ways; it has never been rounded-off with an incontrovertible conclusion, though many people have wrongly assumed that it has. The key task for this book was to find an inarguable underlying truth and end for good the speculation. There have been many twists and turns along the way.

Decades after the war, one of the soldiers who apprehended her in August 1940 recalled how O'Grady's behaviour had aroused his suspicions and how he had twice before warned her not to stray onto the forbidden beach near Sandown. The tearful woman's unsuccessful bid to bribe him and his colleague with money – quite a lot of money – to let her go had done nothing to allay their suspicions. Yet, the attempted bribe apart, O'Grady made no serious attempt to resist arrest that day and, while the army may have harboured little doubt that she was up to no good, there were few local people who subscribed to the same view.

To most of her neighbours in Sandown, Dorothy O'Grady was a bit odd, very reserved with few, if any, friends – but probably harmless. Then again, the very fact that she did seem a bit different from the norm, and had moved to the Isle of Wight only a short time before the war, was probably enough to convince some sections of the civilian population that they had a spy in their midst; perhaps the shadowy, sinister fifth column was at last showing its face.

Certainly, the military had decided to take no chances with O'Grady. They had handed her over to the police and the summonses had quickly followed. On balance, however, it seems improbable that the landlady was regarded by the civilian authorities as anything more than a relatively minor irritant. No attempt was made at this stage to detain her in custody pending her court hearing in Ryde.

The Isle of Wight was on invasion alert, vulnerable to attack, and was being rapidly equipped to defend itself following the British retreat from Dunkirk, the traumatic fall of France, and German occupation of the Channel Islands – all far too close for comfort. Dorothy O'Grady's arrest would serve as an example to others on the 'front line island' that the free and easy days of roaming the beautiful, but now militarily sensitive, coastline of Wight were, at least for the time being, a thing of the past. It was a case of 'bring her in, rap her knuckles, teach her a lesson, let her go' – not a desperately serious situation for Mrs O'Grady.

But her next move in 1940 dramatically changed the whole character of the story.

Bailed to appear before magistrates to answer the two charges against her, she failed to turn up. 'I was too scared to attend,' she would say, after she was tracked down nearly three weeks later. Dorothy O'Grady's flight from justice had taken her to the other end of the island, to the far west seaside village of Totland. It had also transported her from the relatively unimportant status of wartime trespasser to that of a suspected covert enemy agent, actively engaged in various acts of treacherous espionage designed to help the Nazi cause.

Before the year was out, she would be convicted on capital offences at a secret trial in Winchester – and sentenced to death. There is a story that, having said nothing in her defence, she left the courtroom that day with a Nazi salute. That is almost certainly the stuff of legend, but it is not entirely unbelievable. If O'Grady was a frightened innocent, she undoubtedly hid it well. Away from the public gaze, known only to those who were tasked with her custody in the immediate pre-trial period, she had gone out of her way to act the part of a Nazi spy.

Bravado, delusion or plain stupidity?

The arguments that have periodically ever since raged over this extraordinary woman's true wartime status have broadly divided along the same lines: she truly was an enemy agent, actively working for the downfall of Britain; she somehow deluded herself into thinking she was a spy; or she simply pretended to be one.

O'Grady escaped the gallows, instead serving nine years in prison for lesser offences following a successful appeal early in 1941 against her conviction on capital charges brought under the new Treachery Act. She was still an enigma when freed.

Then, over the course of several decades, right up to her death in 1985, she repeatedly fanned the flames of uncertainty with an explanation that was truly bizarre. Interviewed by a series of incredulous journalists, she insisted that she had never been a spy but had very much liked the idea of being thought of as one. It made her feel important – a somebody. So, having been caught in a situation that suggested she might be working for the enemy, she had gone along with it for a bit of fun. A joke. 'The greatest adventure of my life,' she said.

If it all sounded decidedly weird to the journalists who reported her comments, most were convinced it was nothing more sinister. Dorothy O'Grady – jovial, chatty and more than willing to discuss her wartime escapade – was a strange woman.

But a spy? Surely not.

If it had truly been a joke – and that was the version of events she took to the grave – it had come perilously close to costing O'Grady her life. Still, most were prepared to believe her story, content to dismiss her exploits in 1940 as those of a thoroughly bored and lonely woman, deprived by the war of her livelihood as a landlady and the company of her husband, craving excitement and adventure at almost any cost. At most, they surmised, she had been foolish. Very foolish indeed. But, of course, 'dotty Dorothy' could never have been a spy.

Yet, she had clearly convinced the police, the military and even MI5 that she was the real thing, and there were some (myself included) whose minds were not closed to the possibility that she just might have been. Could she have been a lot cleverer than most people thought? Could her 'joke' have been a cover-up? It was possible to argue that O'Grady was in the right place at the right time to have been, potentially at least, an effective agent for the rampaging Third Reich.

That the Isle of Wight was vulnerable to attack in the summer of 1940 had been clearly recognised on either side of the English Channel. Indeed, in July 1940, Hitler had specifically earmarked its possible capture as one way of establishing a foothold on British soil. The broad sweep of Sandown Bay was a tempting landing place for an invasion force and O'Grady was ideally placed in Sandown to provide the sort of information that could prove invaluable in planning such a strike – the location of defensive strongholds, the military strength.

Nobody, apart from O'Grady herself, knew at the time of her many interviews that the account she gave of her life was, in places, short on detail and, in other areas, outright denial of the facts. Whether this was an extension of colourful wartime fantasy or deliberate lies to protect her 'dotty but harmless' image, or whether, in mid and later life, she had simply forgotten some of the key points, divides opinion to this day. Whatever the truth, she died with that image largely intact.

The balance shifted markedly in 1995 when the pages of Britain's national newspapers were splashed with dramatic accounts, compiled from previously undisclosed documents at the Public Record Office (now restyled The National Archives), relating to O'Grady's wartime court hearings, which had been held in camera, with the press and public excluded, such was the sensitivity surrounding her at the time. Those records, locked away, unseen, for more than half a century, seemed to tell a story vastly different from O'Grady's own account.

They told of a woman whose pre-war life had been anything but the humdrum existence she had described. A woman who had already acquired a noteworthy criminal record in the years before her wartime arrest, including convictions before the age of 30 for forgery and theft. The suggestion now was that she had waited years to gain revenge on the British authorities for what she regarded as a wrongful arrest in the 1920s for prostitution. Apparently, she was perceived to have posed such a threat to Britain in 1940 that the then Director of Public Prosecutions was adamant she should hang. Whichever side of the argument over her guilt you adhered to, the documents now in the public domain proved one thing beyond all reasonable doubt: Dorothy O'Grady was a very good storyteller.

Statements from soldiers she had apparently tried to bribe for sensitive information jostled for space in the archived files at the Public Record Office with maps of the Isle of Wight's coastline, highly detailed in O'Grady's own hand with information on gun sites, searchlights, troop positions and concealed transport.

With understandable reasoning, a large section of the British media now condemned O'Grady as 'the supreme mistress of the double bluff, who almost succeeded in helping the Third Reich invade Britain'. The case at last appeared closed.

Doubts subsequently resurfaced. It was quickly, and correctly, pointed out that, despite the raft of 'new' evidence, it could still be argued that the statements, maps and much of the remaining material used to convict O'Grady in 1940 might well have been 'planted' by her, deliberately concocted following her initial arrest, once she had concluded that her coastal meanderings had aroused suspicion or, at the least, some official interest. They might have been part of the elaborate plan she claimed she had dreamt up in order to fool the authorities into thinking she was a genuine spy (and, if that was true, she was worthy of a degree of grudging respect for the extraordinary amount of work she had put into it).

Alternatively, the newly released documents might simply have been evidence of spying delusions. Perhaps she had drawn the maps and bribed the soldiers because she truly thought she was a spy. Possibly that was why, when arrested in Totland, she was found to be using an assumed name – something she tended to play down when giving the last of her colourful press interviews in the 1980s.

Or was her adoption of double-identity merely an extension of her big joke at the authorities' expense? There again, maybe it was another clear sign that she was guilty as charged and desperately trying to evade capture when Totland's village bobbies caught up with her. So run the arguments and counter-arguments.

The media may have decided en masse in 1995 that she had been a traitor, but there are writers of books on Second World War treachery and related topics whose adherence to the opposite view is at least implied. O'Grady was not referred to at all by Sean Murphy in his 2003 round-up of British traitors, *Letting the Side Down*. James Hayward *did* find space for her – briefly – in his *Myths & Legends of the Second World War*, published the same year. 'In December 1940 a landlady named Dorothy O'Grady was sentenced to death for cutting telephone wires on the Isle of Wight, although later it emerged that her confession was false,' he wrote, dismissing the whole thing as a fifth column scare.

Traitor or tease? Or tragically deluded? What was the truth about Dorothy O'Grady? Was it possible to reach a final conclusion or would she forever remain an enigma? The evidence used to convict her in 1940 was, given proper reflection, insufficient to answer any of these questions with a degree of certainty. Her own accounts, the words of a devious storyteller, had to be treated with caution. What was needed was expert opinion on her character and behaviour, and how both may have been influenced by the defining episodes in her pre-war story. Even this might still prove inadequate to reach a decision on whether or not she did betray her country, but it would surely enable a balanced, informed assessment to be made. Was that sort of information available?

It was. A second file of documents relating to Dorothy O'Grady had been compiled. It detailed her prison record before and during the war – and right up to her release from Aylesbury jail, five years early, in 1950. This crucial file promised a wealth of factual information and probable expert analysis on the enigmatic Dorothy, but it had been locked away since the day she walked from Aylesbury and remained hidden from public inspection until a successful application under the Freedom of Information Act secured its release from the Home Office in 2007. Then, just as this vital piece in the O'Grady jigsaw fell into place and I prepared to study the prison papers at The National Archives in Kew, came disturbing news about another major piece of the puzzle. It appeared the Home Office had, months earlier, asked for the temporary return of the initial O'Grady file, containing the documents relating to her trial and conviction, which had been released into the public domain in 1995. That file had never made it back to its allotted storage at Kew. It still hasn't; officially it is 'mislaid'.

Sinister? Mysterious? The questions inevitably have been asked. Was Dorothy O'Grady, posthumously, still managing to pull the strings of her own intrigue?

Fortunately, the newly released prison file did not disappoint. Indeed, it pushed the door wide open on the real Dorothy O'Grady.

The details its long-hidden documents revealed carried her story from the extraordinary to a shocking new level. There had been another, crucial, factor which had driven her so perilously close to the gallows in wartime, a factor unknown to the researchers and theorists who had tried to interpret her life story. It put Dorothy O'Grady into a very distinctive category with few, if any, parallels. Finally, it was possible to reach a conclusion drawn from the full weight of evidential material as to her true status in wartime and throughout a life markedly less ordinary than most.

En route to its conclusion, this book sets out to present the first comprehensive dissection of all the known facts, all the theories and all the legends about Dorothy O'Grady. It examines her personal life and how her childhood and experiences as a young woman undoubtedly *did* influence her later character, behaviour and psychological make-up. It investigates possible links with proven Nazi spies and describes the far from straightforward nature of her imprisonment. The story is not told according to its strict chronology – from birth to the grave – but rather as the facts and changing perceptions of this enduringly fascinating woman emerged during her lifetime and following her death.

Mark Twain's famously oft-quoted idiom that truth is stranger than fiction can seldom have been better applied than in relation to the remarkable story of Dorothy O'Grady.

# 1

# THE SPYING CONTEXT

The process of placing the story of Dorothy O'Grady in its historical context can usefully begin with a summary of German espionage activity within the United Kingdom during the two world wars, together with the measures employed by Britain to deal with suspected covert enemy agents when caught. The eventual fate of those agents – not all of whom suffered the ultimate penalty – adds a further strand of background material to the scene-setting exercise.

Germany's development of a spying ring in the UK prior to the First World War fell victim to an early and highly impressive counter-intelligence coup for Britain's Secret Service Bureau, set up in 1909 principally as a reaction to the alarming growth of German military and naval strength. The fledgling bureau's Home Section was tasked with countering foreign espionage in the UK – in essence, rooting out German agents while its Foreign Section concentrated on gathering secret intelligence abroad. Under the leadership of its first director-general, Captain Vernon Kell, the Home Section (which in 1916 would evolve into Section Five of the newly formed Directorate of Military Intelligence – MI5) swooped on the German spying network as soon as war was declared in August 1914.

With Kell's men acting on information gathered in the pre-war period, the enemy agents were rounded-up and immediately interned. Those caught in the net by the Bureau were the lucky ones. Eleven agents who later arrived in Britain as the war progressed were not so fortunate. All were condemned to death.[1,2]

They were convicted of spying under sections of the Defence of the Realm Act, which had entered the statute books a matter of days after the war's declaration. Most were tried by military courts martial, though two faced criminal proceedings at the Central Criminal Court (Old Bailey) in London. All eleven were executed by firing squad at the Tower of London between November 1914 and April 1916 – either in the miniature rifle range, since demolished, or in the Tower ditch. No women suffered the same fate, though Swedish-born Eva de Bournonville came perilously close when she was sentenced to death at the Old Bailey in January 1916 for attempting to communicate sensitive information to the enemy. Reprieved on appeal, she then served six years in prison.

The legislation ushered in under the Defence of the Realm Act (popularly known as DORA) had provided the government with a raft of powers designed to meet the threat posed by the first official 'state of national emergency' in Britain since the Napoleonic Wars of 1799–1815. The Act allowed the introduction of wide-ranging regulations in pursuit of public safety and the nation's defence in wartime. It paved the way for the drafting of new legislation in the immediate post-war period permitting the government to retain on a more permanent basis the right to impose the sort of sanctions hitherto reserved for wartime. Becoming law in 1920, this was known as the Emergency Powers Act.

Introduced by Lloyd George's coalition government, the Act allowed a state of emergency to be declared whenever, in Parliament's opinion, the nation's essential services were threatened. The most noteworthy – and prolonged – use of the Act in the interwar years came at the time of the General Strike in 1926, when it was in force for a considerably longer period than the few days of the strike itself – after Stanley Baldwin's Conservative administration forced the trades union movement's general surrender, leaving the miners to soldier on alone.

Thus, the core legislation was already in place when war again threatened between Britain and Germany in the late 1930s. With the nation's security once more at risk, Prime Minister Neville Chamberlain successfully sought parliamentary approval in August 1939 for an Emergency Powers (Defence) Act. Becoming law on the 24th of that month, one day after the alarming news of Germany's non-aggression pact with the Soviet Union, it armed the British Government with the powers to take whatever measures it saw fit to secure public safety, defend the nation and maintain order. Within a week of the Act coming into force, more than 100 new measures had been introduced. Split into several sections, they were known collectively as the Defence Regulations.[3, 4]

Most of these wide-ranging measures were covered by the Defence (General) Regulations, though others with narrower, specific objectives were separately introduced. 'Headline' uses included the call-up of military reservists and the mobilisation of Air Raid Precautions (ARP) volunteers. A number of Defence Regulations, designed principally to prevent spying activity and interference with essential services, imposed a series of restrictions on the civilian population. It was alleged breaches of these that would first bring Dorothy O'Grady to the attention of the military and civilian authorities in the summer of 1940.

Once they had taken a rather more serious view of her activities, following the three weeks O'Grady spent on the run from justice, the Crown prosecutors added more sinister-sounding counts to an expanding sheet that would eventually run to nine charges. Now believing that she had not merely trespassed on the forbidden foreshore but had acted in a manner prejudicial to the interests of the State and carried out specific acts which threatened national security, the Crown was able to look to the Official Secrets Act of 1911 to aid its prosecution.

However, although she was prosecuted for breaches of both the Defence Regulations and Official Secrets Act, it was the capital charges she faced under the Treachery Act of 1940 that very nearly took the Isle of Wight landlady to the gallows.

The Treachery Act became law on 23 May 1940, thirteen days after Winston Churchill succeeded the disillusioned Chamberlain as prime minister and four days before the first Allied soldiers would miraculously escape the horrors of Dunkirk. With the enemy at the door – or very close to it – and soon planning to break it down via cross-Channel invasion, the Act was a timely, tough new measure to safeguard national security by the capture and prosecution of enemy agents.

Unlike the requirements for the Treason Act of 1351 (which still applied in 1940 and would be employed successfully five years later to convict the infamous Nazi broadcaster William Joyce, Lord Haw-Haw), prosecutions brought under the Treachery Act had no need to establish whether a defendant owed allegiance to the Head of State in order to find him or her guilty. To secure a conviction, it was sufficient only to show that he or she 'with intent to help the enemy ... does, or attempts, or conspires with any other person, to do, any act which is designed or likely to give assistance to the naval, military or air operations of the enemy, to impede such operations of His Majesty's forces, or to endanger life.'

This somewhat convoluted definition of the 1940 Act's scope and purpose was at odds with the simplicity of outcome for anyone convicted under its terms. The mandatory sentence in all cases was death. Dorothy O'Grady was the first Briton of either sex to be condemned to death under the Treachery Act. Had her February 1941 appeal not saved her from the gallows, she would have been the only woman of any nationality to suffer death under the Act during the Second World War – indeed, the only woman executed in Britain for spying in the entire twentieth century.

Seventeen men *did* suffer that fate between December 1940, the month of O'Grady's trial in Winchester, and January 1946, the year after the war's conclusion. Most stood trial under the Treachery Act before a judge and jury at the Old Bailey, though two were convicted by military courts martial. All but one were hanged in London prisons – either at Pentonville or Wandsworth. The single exception was Josef Jakobs (43), whose spying mission in England had ended before it had a chance to begin when he parachuted from the aircraft that had brought him from Holland, broke an ankle on landing and was quickly captured by the local Home Guard near Ramsey in the wilds of Huntingdonshire. Tried by court martial, he was sentenced to a military execution. On 15 August 1941 he became the last of the many people across the centuries to suffer execution at the Tower of London when he was shot by a firing squad in the miniature rifle range. It is a distinction he seems destined to retain.

As with the Jakobs case, the majority of convicted enemy agents executed in Britain during the Second World War were foreign nationals. The handful of British subjects who met the same fate were all tried for espionage activity carried out abroad. Had Dorothy O'Grady's appeal failed, she would have been the only Briton executed during the war for treachery committed within the UK.

Newcastle-born marine engineer George Armstrong (39), hanged at Wandsworth in July 1941, was convicted on evidence that, while in the USA with his merchant ship during November 1940, he wrote to the German Consul in Boston, Massachusetts, offering his services, information and assistance to the enemy. A convicted con man, Armstrong's later claim that he had done so in an attempt to expose a pro-German spying network in the States failed to save his life.

Merchant seaman Duncan Scott-Ford, from Plymouth, was hanged at Wandsworth in November 1942 for supplying secret information to Germany on vital shipping convoy movements between Britain and Portugal – not his first espionage mission in the enemy's interests. Initially paid for his treachery, he was subsequently blackmailed in Lisbon by agents of the Nazis, whose threats to expose him to the British authorities forced his continued compliance with their demands. The highly impressionable Scott-Ford, who had earlier been dismissed from the Royal Navy at a court martial and served six months in prison for forgery and embezzlement, was just 21 at the time of his execution.

London-born Theodore Schurch (whose father was Swiss) became the last enemy agent to suffer execution when he was hanged at Pentonville in January 1946. Schurch was cajoled into enlisting with the British armed forces by Italian fascists before the war with the express purpose of passing militarily sensitive information to his Italian spymasters. He became an effective agent for Italy in the Middle East during the early years of the war. Allowing himself to be captured by the Germans at the Libyan port of Tobruk in June 1942, he resumed contact with Italian intelligence. Schurch spent the best part of the next three years seeking out information for Italy and then the German SS – notably from British prisoners of war – before his treachery ran its course in March 1945 when he was arrested by the Americans in Rome. At his court martial in London, Schurch (27) was found guilty of both treachery and desertion.

The fourth convicted traitor with British citizenship, thanks to his birth in Gibraltar thirty-four years earlier, was Jose Key, who was hanged at Wandsworth in July 1942 after a search on the Rock revealed him to be in possession of sensitive military information. Key, it was later proven, was planning to transmit this to the enemy.

Oswald Job, some of whose treachery did take place in the UK, was the only other British-born Nazi agent among the seventeen executed men. However, although he started life in London and was educated at an English public school, both his parents were German. Job's route to the gallows at Pentonville in March 1944 began when he was interned by the Germans in occupied France because of his British passport. Managing to convince the occupying force of his German credentials, he returned to Britain via Spain. Having aroused suspicions in the UK, Job's fate was sealed with the discovery of invisible ink crystals, cipher material and other spying paraphernalia which he had concealed within a large bunch of hollowed keys and in the handle of his safety razor. At 59, Oswald Job was the oldest of the seventeen men to suffer the death penalty under the Treachery Act.

So far, as female involvement in pro-Nazi espionage activity on British soil is concerned, the star billing in the Second World War undoubtedly belonged to the vivacious and enduringly mysterious Vera Schalburg – despite the fact that her spying mission in the UK appears to have been an abject failure. Better remembered in Britain as Vera Eriksson, the Danish alias she was using at the time, Schalburg arrived in September 1940 with two male colleagues in the north-east of Scotland. The trio's planned journey south for spying roles in London was thwarted by speedy capture – a fitting end for a shambolic, ill-planned mission. The three agents' subsequent arrest, the trial and execution of the two men, Vera's escape from justice and the mystery of her ultimate fate have fascinated historians for decades. The release in recent years of wartime MI5 files relating to the woman dubbed 'the beautiful spy' threw considerable light on her background and involvement with Nazi Germany, but questions remain.

The very fact that so much of the mystery and argument over this fascinating Russian-born woman continues to this day means that, in this respect at least, her story has a parallel in the O'Grady case. In fact, there are further similarities between the two, although coincidences might seem the more appropriate term considering the vastly different circumstances that provide the bulk of the background to their life stories. Like Vera Schalburg, Dorothy O'Grady was adopted as an infant (see Chapter 8) and only a matter of weeks separated their respective police arrests in the early autumn of 1940. But could there be a *real* link?

It may seem fanciful to suggest a closer association between the two women, but there is both firm evidence and apparently well-founded theory to support the notion that there might have been. Historical fact can place them under the same roof on at least two occasions during the war and, amazingly, there is a suggestion that they might also have lived as near neighbours, relatively speaking, in the years *after* the war – on the Isle of Wight. Whatever the underlying truth, it is at least a remarkable coincidence that the island should be linked, however tenuously in the case of Schalburg, to both of these leading female characters in the annals of German spying folklore of the Second World War.

The possible link between Schalburg and O'Grady may be regarded as the stuff of whimsy but it is nonetheless worthy of closer scrutiny. It is examined fully in later chapters.[5]

Schalburg and her companions were caught out by inadequate preparation and inefficient implementation – not, it would seem, by any secret intelligence that warned MI5 in advance of their mission in Britain. The deservedly well-documented success of the Security Service (MI5's official title since 1931) in uncovering supposedly covert enemy agents did not blossom until 1941. MI5 then became so adept at this that it was able to turn most of the spies sent to Britain by Germany against their former Nazi spymasters and the Third Reich as a whole. So successful was Britain's famous Double-Cross System that J.C. Masterman, who chaired the committee in charge of it, felt able to conclude that 'we actively ran and controlled the German espionage system in this country'.[6]

MI5 files released in recent years to Britain's National Archives confirmed that the extraordinary success of the Double-Cross System was achieved via a combination of counter-espionage work before the war and signals intelligence during it. The Security Service was able to monitor the deployment of German agents and, consequently, pick them up more or less on their arrival in the UK. If they couldn't be 'turned' – as was evidently the case with Vera Schalburg's two male colleagues – they faced the unpalatable consequences of trial and a mandatory death sentence under the Treachery Act. The vast majority became double agents.

The pressure on them to turn against their German controllers was intense. Following capture, the agents faced interrogation at Latchmere House on Ham Common in south London, the formidable, specially adapted MI5 detention centre known in wartime as Camp 020. In all, 480 people were interned there for periods during the Second World War. Nazi agents arriving from occupied Europe provided the principal source of 'raw material' for MI5's interrogators but there were others – suspected of either working for German interests or harbouring sympathies for the enemy – who passed through the less than welcoming doors of Camp 020.[7]

There is no doubt that MI5 took a keen interest in Dorothy O'Grady after her military arrest and subsequent dash from justice in August 1940. They could hardly have done otherwise. Why had she run away? Until then, however, there is no evidence to suggest that she had roused the suspicions of the Security Service.

Did she harbour fascist sympathies? Most Britons who did were either interned in the UK during the war or – in the cases of those who were the most committed to Hitlerian doctrine and, more often than not, were rabid anti-Semitists – had got out of the country in time to spend the war years in Germany or elsewhere, broadcasting propaganda or actively pursuing other work in the enemy's cause. O'Grady, of course, was imprisoned rather than interned and her war effort for the enemy – if it truly existed – was wholly on British shores. There is some evidence, entirely self-professed, that she may have been an admirer of Hitler, but this has usually been dismissed – as eventually it was by her – as nothing more than a further extension of fantasy or delusion.

Despite the unprecedented success it would later achieve, the Security Service had begun the war in a state of near-chaos. It was understaffed and unprepared for the huge increase in its workload brought about by the need to respond to the avalanche of requests for vetting people suspected of posing a threat to the nation's security. The demand was exacerbated by the mood of a nervous nation.

Treachery was everywhere in the early part of the war. That, at least, was the perception of a jittery British public. Suspicion among the populace suited a government anxious to avoid sensitive information reaching the ears of the enemy. Striking posters from the Ministry of Information hammered home the dire consequences of 'careless talk' and would soon be reminding would-be blabbers to 'keep it under your hat' – but just about anyone who seemed, in appearance, background or behaviour, to be out of the ordinary stood the risk of being seen as a potential traitor or spy. The sinister term 'fifth columnist' had entered the language.

In the Second World War, fifth columnist became a 'catch all' phrase for Nazi agents and collaborators secretly carrying out subversive operations in targeted nations. It had originated a few years earlier during the Spanish Civil War – specifically the October 1936 Siege of Madrid by four columns of Nationalist troops under the command of General Emilio Mola. In the course of a broadcast for a rebel radio station, the general trumpeted that he would be able to call on additional supporters hiding within the city to reinforce the Fascist cause. It remains a matter of debate whether it was Mola himself or, more likely, the US press reporting the war who first tagged this shadowy force the fifth column. Mola's move on the Spanish capital failed and the following June he was killed in a plane crash. But the fifth column was set to transcend the Civil War.

There was a widely held belief that the Germans' lightning advance across western Europe in 1940 could not possibly have been achieved without some form of organised, embedded support for the Nazi forces within the nations that successively capitulated to the might of Hitler's stunning Blitzkrieg offensive. And, ran the near-hysterical argument in Britain, if a fifth column had existed in Scandinavia, the Low Countries and France, then why not here in the UK as well?

The Germans' substantial employment of paratroops for the invasion of Holland early in May 1940 was a particularly rich source of rumour and falsehood. With sinister reports reaching Britain of parachuted enemy troops dropping from the sky dressed variously as clergymen, peasants and Dutch forces, it was hardly surprising that the same newspaper accounts told of 'hundreds of fifth column suspects' being rounded-up in the UK as a precaution.[8]

It is a moot point whether or not the perceived threat and fear of a fascist fifth column in Britain – a spy on every corner – led to more harm than the actual existence of one would have posed. There is certainly no doubt that it fuelled suspicion in the UK and the circumstances surrounding the Dorothy O'Grady affair cannot be properly considered without due regard being accorded to its impact.

# Notes

1   Vernon Kell was still in post as the head of MI5 when hostilities with Germany were renewed in 1939, by which time he had been given the army rank of major general. Winston Churchill, vociferously critical of MI5's

leadership and, indeed, its overall competence, relieved him of his duties in June 1940 soon after becoming prime minister. Vernon Kell was knighted before his death in March 1942.

2   Before becoming part of the new Directorate of Military Intelligence, MI5, in September 1916, the Secret Service Bureau's Home Section had already been absorbed into the War Office for the duration of the First World War, initially becoming part of Section Five within the Directorate of Military Operations – MO5(g).

3   Formally the Treaty of Non-aggression between Germany and the Union of Soviet Socialist Republics, the agreement is often recalled as the Hitler–Stalin Pact and, more commonly, as the Molotov–Ribbentrop Pact after the two Foreign Ministers who signed it in Moscow on behalf of their respective nations – the USSR's Vyacheslav Molotov and Nazi Germany's Joachim von Ribbentrop. It was abruptly terminated in June 1941 following Operation Barbarossa, Germany's invasion of the Soviet Union.

4   A second Emergency Powers (Defence) Act, introduced in 1940, extended the use of Defence Regulations into areas such as industrial conscription.

5   Vera Schalburg had a string of aliases. There were almost as many optional spellings of her real surname. She was variously known (or is recalled today) as Schalberg, Chalburg, Chqlbur, Erikson, Eriksson, Eriksen, Erichsen, De Cottani, Von Wedel and Starizky. She may have lived under another alias after the war.

6   John Cecil Masterman (1891–1977). The quoted extract is from his book *The Double Cross System in the War of 1939 to 1945*, compiled immediately after the war but not published until 1972 after the British Government repeatedly blocked its release, forcing Masterman to find a publisher (Yale University Press) in the USA – beyond the reach of Britain's Official Secrets Act and MI5's sensitivities.

7   Latchmere House acquired a fearsome reputation after the war when parallels with Gestapo methods of interrogation in Germany were drawn by some former internees. When MI5 released files in 1999 on Latchmere's wartime role, the documents confirmed that considerable psychological pressure to co-operate had been brought to bear on Camp 020's inmates, but the released files also included MI5's insistence that at no time was physical torture or violence employed against any of the internees.

8   Hayward, James, *Myths & Legends of the Second World War* (Sutton, 2003).

2

# AN ENEMY TARGET:
# A VULNERABLE ISLAND

That the Isle of Wight should have found itself on invasion alert in the summer of 1940 was entirely in keeping with the broad brush of its eventful history. Over the course of many centuries, the island's vulnerability to invasion from continental Europe had been amply, and destructively, demonstrated on innumerable occasions. Unsurprisingly, the threat from the latter period of the Middle Ages onwards came usually from neighbouring France, whose countrymen not infrequently found the island, just adrift from England's south coast, a reachable and irresistible magnet for seaborne assault – and a potential stepping stone for an all-out invasion of the mother country a few miles beyond.

The frequency and ferocity of French-led attacks on the Isle of Wight in the fourteenth and fifteenth centuries, during the Hundred Years War, brought desolation and demoralisation on an unprecedented scale. That the island managed somehow to resist total capitulation was little short of miraculous. It came perilously close in 1377 when the French, aided by Castilian forces, launched devastating raids against the ports of Yarmouth and Newtown, on the isle's north-west coast, and laid lengthy siege to the inland defensive stronghold of Carisbrooke Castle.

In the sixteenth century Henry VIII equipped the Isle of Wight far better to defend itself – together with the Solent sea lanes which separate it from mainland England – through the construction of a string of coastal fortifications on the island's northern and eastern shorelines, and along the Hampshire coast on the other side of the water. However, it was not until the second half of the nineteenth century that a renewed threat of French aggression brought about the next meaningful defensive modernisation. The chief aim in the building of new coastal gun batteries and forts either side of the sea – plus the four imposing sea forts which continue to dominate the eastern Solent, like a quartet of stranded whales, to this day – was not directly concerned with the security of Wight. The principal consideration was to help defend both approaches to the Solent, east and west, together with the Royal Navy's Spithead anchorage, lying just off Portsmouth, and the city's strategically vital naval harbour and dockyard.[1,2]

Further gun batteries followed in the first decade of the twentieth century to beef up defensive capabilities around the Isle of Wight's north-east coast – the 'front door' to the Solent and Portsmouth's naval installations – but many of the island's coastal fortifications were 'mothballed' on a care and maintenance basis in the decades before the outbreak of war with Nazi Germany. Reactivation of some of the old defences was triggered by the rapidly worsening international situation in 1938 but, in a somewhat ironic twist of fate given the historical legacy, it took the desperate retreat of the British Expeditionary Force from Dunkirk in May 1940, the inevitability of French surrender and the enemy's occupation of the Channel Islands shortly afterwards to equip the Isle of Wight with the means to offer any sort of meaningful resistance against Hitler's Blitzkrieg.

Up until that momentous point in the war, the island had not been regarded by the British Government as particularly vulnerable to German attack – despite repeated protestations from local officials dismayed at the lack of Whitehall cash support for large-scale air-raid shelter provision and other protective measures for islanders. Given the scope of mid-twentieth-century warfare – particularly from the air – it seemed palpably obvious to the island's inhabitants that their homeland would be left perilously exposed to the highest risk of danger by its close proximity both to Portsmouth and the commercial docks and shipyards at Southampton. Added to this, the island had its own major shipbuilding and aircraft production concerns located at the port of Cowes. The people of Wight knew it was vulnerable – no matter what the government was saying.

So the Isle of Wight had prepared for war as best it could by developing a level of civil defence efficiency, which even London acknowledged compared favourably with that in many other parts of the country. Yet, a year after Neville Chamberlain's promise of 'peace for our time' had proved not to be worth the infamous piece of paper on which it was based, and with the declaration of war in September 1939 just days away, the island found itself serving as a reception centre for schoolchildren, evacuated from the nearby mainland to offshore protection in what the Home Office had declared a 'safe haven' relatively free of danger.

It was little short of a farce and many parents in Portsmouth and Gosport, whose children had been earmarked to travel to the island in their droves, recognised it as such, preferring to keep their offspring at home rather than send them a few miles across the water on a thirty-minute ferry trip. A large number of those who did make the crossing quickly returned when the near pointlessness of the exercise became clear. The Isle of Wight was never a safe haven.

The only plausible reason for this muddled thinking on the part of the Home Office was the widely held belief that, if threatened, France would be strong enough to resist the Nazi onslaught. Therefore, any large-scale assault on Britain would more likely come via the east coast of England, rather than the south. Even so, it still had the look of a horribly misjudged bit of national policy – and so it was to prove. The Isle of Wight was destined for a very active war.

The traumatic collapse of France was, of course, the catalyst. The expensively assembled Maginot Line of defensive fortifications on the eastern French border with Germany was largely side-stepped by the Wehrmacht's brutal violation of neutrality in the Low Countries, allowing an attack from the north and confounding any perceived pre-war wisdom of Gallic impregnability. The rampaging enemy had the island, whose southern shores now faced them, firmly in their target sights in the summer of 1940 – and for more than one reason.

In July 1940, Adolf Hitler's declaration of intent to bring the United Kingdom to its knees through a seaborne invasion from the French coast, and the growing awareness in Britain that this was more than a realistic possibility, catapulted to prominence, on both sides of the English Channel, the obvious vulnerability of the Isle of Wight, which the press were now calling the 'front line island'.

Having overseen the rapid achievement of his military ambitions in western Europe, an impatient Hitler, despairing of stand-alone Britain's refusal to show any 'willingness to come to an agreement in spite of her hopeless military situation', ordered preparations for a hitherto unscheduled invasion and, if necessary, occupation of Britain. Operation Sea Lion soon became a reality – at least in planning terms – with Hitler proposing an amphibious assault in the form of 'a surprise crossing on a broad front extending approximately from Ramsgate to the region of the Isle of Wight'. His directive added, 'Each individual branch of the Wehrmacht will examine from its own viewpoint whether it appears practicable to carry out subsidiary operations, for example to occupy the Isle of Wight or the county of Cornwall, prior to the general crossing ...'[3]

Had Hitler's suggested initial occupation of the island gone ahead there seems little doubt that the principal invasion beach would have been Sandown Bay on the island's south-east coast. The broad, level sweep of the bay was an ideal landing place. How serious a proposition this preliminary strike – indeed, the entire operation – truly was is a matter for conjecture. Hitler, it is argued, might have been bluffing, ordering full-scale preparations in a bid to frighten a weakened Britain into an outright surrender or a negotiated rapprochement with Germany. Or did he view invasion as a contingency for use only as a very last resort?

Whatever the Führer's true intentions in July 1940, the Wehrmacht took the prospect of invasion seriously enough. Army strategists had already drawn up plans for an assault broadly in tune with Hitler's outline – landings across a 200-mile expanse of southern England coastline from Ramsgate in the east to the Dorset resort of Lyme Regis in the west. While the prospects for capturing either the Isle of Wight or Cornwall prior to the main invasion had not featured in the Wehrmacht's planning, the island was specifically earmarked as one of several probable landing sites on that initial army blueprint for the main assault.

Divisions of the German 9th Army, part of Field Marshal Gerd von Rundstedt's Army Group A in the envisaged assault formation, would be assigned the Isle of Wight landing mission, having crossed from Le Havre, while other units of the same force headed from the Normandy port to the area of Brighton. The Channel would also be crossed from Cherbourg and Calais, either side of the Le Havre route, with targeted landings on the western and eastern flanks of the assault.

Information on the precise landing sites was vague (if properly considered at all), though the interpretation of some today that Ventnor, in the south-east corner of the island – thus marginally closest to Le Havre – was the chosen location on the Isle of Wight is either wide of the mark or indicative of very shoddy German forethought. The town is built on steeply graded terraces in a narrow gap between the island's highest hills and the sea, hardly ideal break-out territory for an invasion force which would first have to avoid rocky coastline in close proximity. Had the arrows snaking across the Channel on the Wehrmacht's plans in the direction of southern Wight translated into reality, the landing beach would clearly have been a few miles further north in Sandown Bay.[4,5]

The German army was cockily confident of overall success. The German navy was horrified. Grand Admiral Erich Raeder and his senior colleagues, worried about the twin threats posed by the strength of the Royal Navy and the presence of sea mines in the Channel, insisted that invasion on such a wide front, necessitating lengthy and particularly hazardous sea crossings in the west, was far too risky. They wanted an assault on a much narrower front, concentrated on the shortest Channel crossing, from Calais, in the east. Eventually, in August 1940, compromise was reached and the final plans for Operation Sea Lion envisaged landings between Folkestone and Selsey Bill, west of Brighton, with no further serious consideration given either to attacking or capturing the Isle of Wight.

It is, however, pertinent to note, in the context of Dorothy O'Grady's alleged spying activity, that right up to the month of her initial military arrest the island was still a possible German objective – and might conceivably have remained so.

As the inter-service arguments raged between the highest levels of the German military, the Isle of Wight was at last being equipped to withstand, or at least hamper, the potential arrival of the enemy on its shores. Operation Sea Lion would eventually fall victim to the failure of the Luftwaffe to first achieve the essential prerequisite of aerial supremacy in the Battle of Britain – a significant proportion of which was fought in the skies above the island – but in the summer of 1940, on the English side of the Channel, a Nazi invasion of the Isle of Wight could not be ruled out. Secret intelligence reports had suggested that it had been under consideration The threat was being taken very seriously indeed.

The *Isle of Wight County Press* might have sought to allay local fears back in early June by asserting that 'it would be exceedingly difficult for an enemy to attack the Isle of Wight in any strength', but within days any comfort its readers may have taken from this had been nullified by all too obvious signs of the enemy's proximity and the measures that would be adopted to keep them out.

High-explosive bombs started falling on the Isle of Wight on 16 June, two days after Hitler's triumphant forces had entered Paris – and exactly one week after the arrival on the island of an infantry brigade to form an initial garrison force. With coastal defence the immediate priority, the island's metamorphosis from seaside retreat to fortress quickly gathered pace as the newly arrived soldiers ringed the coastline with a variety of anti-invasion obstacles. A year after inviting thousands of visitors to sample their typically English pleasures in the final pre-war summer, seaside piers on the 'holiday coast' at Sandown, Shanklin and Ventnor were now made as uninviting as possible for a visit from the enemy by the expedient of having the middle sections of their decking removed.[6]

While reactivation and/or rearmament of the Victorian gun batteries (and the construction of a new battery at Bouldnor, in the north-west) provided the principal coastal protection, supported by smaller emplacements and a rash of 'pill box' positions, the island's interior was equipped in 1940 with the significant deterrent of heavy anti-aircraft gun sites manned by the Royal Artillery. Unlike the demilitarised Channel Islands to the south, taken by the Germans on 30 June, the Isle of Wight was progressively, if hastily, attired in the full panoply of war. Security had tightened. To travel to or from the island required a special permit. The 'right to roam' was severely curtailed. The holiday beaches were out of bounds. The new Defence Regulations had begun to bite.

Put in the countryside, small groups of men familiar with the contours and features of the landscape – farmers, farm labourers, gamekeepers, etc. – were soon working by moonlight in the utmost secrecy to dig concealed underground hideouts. Stocked with emergency rations, weaponry and ammunition, these subterranean chambers would become their living quarters if, despite the defensive measures to prevent it, the German jackboot made it ashore.

Named with deliberate vagueness the Auxiliary Units of the Home Guard, the specially recruited volunteers signed the Official Secrets Act and were trained in the irregular tactics of guerilla warfare, ready to perform the seriously hazardous duties of a stay-behind force on what would be an otherwise virtually deserted island – harrying for as long as they could from behind the lines the enemy's break-out from the beach. Ambush, sabotage and intelligence-gathering were their allotted tasks. The Isle of Wight was among the first of the country's 'at risk' locations to develop what effectively was the English resistance.[7]

The potential for invasion was a major reason for enemy interest in the Isle of Wight, but not the only one. As noted, the island possessed several 'legitimate' targets of warfare. The key strategic target for the Luftwaffe in the summer of 1940 was St Boniface Down, in the south-east of the island – its highest hill at 791ft. On it stood RAF Ventnor, a vital link in the initial chain of radar stations located around the coast of south-eastern England. It was the furthest west of the original sixteen Radio Direction Finding (the name by which radar was first known) installations, developed amid great secrecy in the years before the war.

The station, with its eight tall pylons (later reduced to seven) for transmitter aerials and receivers, had dominated the high-level landscape (as well as local gossip and fanciful imagination) after coming on stream at the end of January 1939 as the first of several radar installations, operated by one or other of the three armed services, that would be located on the Isle of Wight during the six years of war. Radar was crucial to the defence of the nation against the Luftwaffe.

Two devastating attacks on RAF Ventnor by enemy planes on 12 and 16 August 1940, temporarily knocking it out of operation, amounted to the most significant enemy action against the Isle of Wight's strategic targets in the period prior to Dorothy O'Grady's emergence as a suspected enemy agent, sandwiched as they were between the dates of her military arrest on the beach at Yaverland and the appointment that she failed to keep with the magistrates at Ryde.[8]

In the twin towns of Cowes and East Cowes, separated by the River Medina at the island's northern-most point, the large industrial firms of J. Samuel White's and Saunders-Roe were regarded from the start as important contributors – of warships and amphibious aircraft, respectively – to the wartime production line in the UK. It was an importance that would not be lost on the enemy as the war progressed. During May 1942, after a particularly heavy, two-pronged overnight raid on the towns caused markedly more damage and loss of life than any other single incident in the island's war, Axis propagandists would have a 'field day' as newspapers in both Germany and Italy reproduced aerial photographs of the bomb damage in what they called 'the industrial centre of Britain'.[9]

It was, of course, an exaggeration, but between June 1940 and November 1944 islanders would be alerted approximately 1,600 times to the presence of enemy aircraft in their midst. This tally of air-raid alerts was among the highest in the country.[10]

That did not mean that the Luftwaffe spent a disproportionate amount of time attacking Isle of Wight targets, but the island and its coastal waters lay beneath the flight path of countless enemy aircraft bound for objectives in southern England and beyond. It was a convenient dumping ground for bomber crews whose planes, having been intercepted by the RAF's Hurricanes and Spitfires, had turned tail and found their unused bombs something of a cumbersome hindrance in the race back to the safety of their captured airfields in occupied France.

By the end of the war, the number of air raids specifically targeted against the Isle of Wight by the Luftwaffe would reach 125 (the first in June 1940; the last in July 1944). They would contribute to the 1,728 bombs (excluding countless incendiaries) that rained down on the island, killing 214 civilians (ninety-two men, ninety women and twelve children) and seriously injuring a further 274. Across the island, 10,873 buildings would be damaged by enemy action, 552 of them beyond repair.

From the start, the enemy's fighter and bomber crews had plenty of information about the island at their disposal. Ahead of the field, by 1940 Nazi Germany's military intelligence had furnished the Luftwaffe and its sister forces with a comprehensive archive of aerial reconnaissance material covering the whole of the British Isles. The Isle of Wight's coastline was extensively photographed, its military, industrial and transport facilities marked on the resultant pictures and on Ordnance Survey maps. Together with hand-drawn coastal profiles, this key information was packaged in what amounted to a useful handbook for attack.

There was, of course, no barrier in the pre-war years to German nationals collecting material of potential military value by the simple expedients of taking photographs, purchasing maps, guidebooks and picture postcards, and committing to memory features of the landscape while on holiday in the UK. Visiting sportsmen in particular were officially encouraged to do so. 'It could be useful to the Fatherland one day' was the gist of the message from the Nazi regime. It is a moot point whether or not this readily available form of intelligence gathering was the real reason behind visits made by groups of young tourists to the Isle of Wight and other areas of the country in 1937. MI5 suspected it might have been. The teenage tourists were members of the Hitler Youth.

Files released recently to The National Archives reveal the Security Service's concern that a series of cycling holidays in the UK organised by the Nazi youth branch was convenient cover for espionage rather than a desire to foster links with Britain's Boy Scouts movement, which the German officials were keen to portray as the prime motivation behind them. MI5's decision to ask UK police forces to keep an eye on the young Germans was partly fuelled by a report in the *Daily Herald* suggesting that the teenage Nazis were under orders to gather information. The headline – 'NAZIS MUST BE SPYCLISTS' – left no room for doubt.[11]

On the Isle of Wight the 'spyclists' were based at The Hermitage, the island's first youth hostel, on the top of St Catherine's Down, a lofty perch for the eagle-eyed youngsters, overlooking the English Channel near the island's southern-most point. Not a bad place to roost if spying was their undercover game.[12]

Yet, the intelligence gained by Germany about the Isle of Wight in the years leading up to the outbreak of war was useful only up to a point. In the summer of 1940 things were changing so rapidly that much of the pre-war information was rendered obsolete, or in urgent need of updating and reassessment. Given the existence of the isle's strategic targets, the possibilities offered by Sandown Bay for invasion and the island's sheer vulnerability to attack and occupation, it is easy to argue that this was a location rich in potential for an active enemy agent, especially one whose home was handily placed just above the sweep of the bay and directly across the road from the army garrison at Sandown Barracks.[13]

## Notes

1. One of the Henrician fortifications on the Isle of Wight coast, the vastly altered West Cowes Castle, headquarters of the prestigious Royal Yacht Squadron, saw military use in the Second World War. Offered to the Admiralty, it became HMS *Vectis*, a base for Combined Operations, reverting to the RYS after the war. Yarmouth Castle is the only other of the island's Tudor fortresses surviving today, preserved as an ancient monument in the care of English Heritage. East Cowes Castle and Sandham Castle (Sandown) succumbed centuries ago to the rigours of coastal erosion. No visible traces remain of either.

2. Use in the Second World War of the nineteenth-century sea forts (St Helens, No Man's Land, Horse Sand and Spit Bank, in order of their proximity to the Isle of Wight) was largely restricted to searchlight and light anti-aircraft roles. No Man's Land and Horse Sand were additionally linked to a submerged cross-Solent submarine boom net defence, while Spit Bank was assigned an important ship monitoring role within Portsmouth's inner defences and kept a look-out for mines parachuted into the sea by enemy planes.

3. Führer Directive No. 16 (16 July 1940): 'Preparations for the invasion of Britain.'

4. The primary objective of the landings was to achieve an initial bridgehead along the coast from Portsmouth to Ramsgate.

5. A communications misunderstanding on Saturday 7 September 1940 led to the issuing along England's south coast of the coded alert for a German invasion – Cromwell. Sandown Bay's defensive positions, manned to a large extent by mobilised Home Guardsmen under Regular Army direction, remained on high alert throughout the weekend before the situation was clarified. This dramatic false alarm took place while Dorothy O'Grady was being pursued by the police after her failure to attend court.

6. This anti-invasion measure did not apply to the much longer Ryde Pier further north because of its vital role in conveying – by train, tram or on foot – cross-Solent passengers to and from the Portsmouth ferries.

7. The locations of several of the island's secret underground hideouts, deserted at the end of the war, have since been revealed, usually due to the collapse of

their concealed roofs. Built principally in woodland, their function – and that of the Auxiliary Units themselves – remained a secret until the 1960s.

8  Apart from damaging the pylons themselves, the two attacks on the radar station on 12 and 16 August – both part of wider Luftwaffe offensives against RAF targets in southern England – rendered virtually all the service buildings, above and below ground, unusable. The island's vital link in the radar chain was restored on 23 August with the opening of a small temporary reserve facility on Bembridge Down.

9  The May 1942 blitz on Cowes and East Cowes caused seventy civilian deaths in the twin towns and a further ten in the area of Newport. Many others were seriously injured and there was extensive damage to homes.

10  Some sources have suggested that only Dover, with 3,059, had a greater number of air-raid alerts.

11  The *Daily Herald*'s article quoted instructions purportedly from the Nazi government which, the newspaper reported, had appeared in a German cycling journal. Readers visiting Britain and other foreign countries were urged in the translated version to 'make a note of the names of places, rivers, seas and mountains. Perhaps you may be able to utilise these sometime for the benefit of the Fatherland.'

12  St Catherine's Point, overlooked by the high chalk downs at the island's southern tip, was the area originally earmarked for the radar station which eventually opened slightly to the east on St Boniface Down. Had the initial location plan not been changed, The Hermitage, built in the early nineteenth century atop St Catherine's Down, would have been a near – possibly a very near – neighbour of the radar station.

13  While Sandown Barracks was militarily active as a garrison during the war, its nineteenth-century battery, on the opposite (seaward) side of Broadway, very close to Dorothy O'Grady's house, was not in operational use. The barracks, vacated by the army in the early 1950s, now provide office accommodation for the Isle of Wight Council behind The Heights Leisure Centre, which opened in 1982.

# 3

# No More Milk till
# I Return

Relatively few people on the Isle of Wight knew of the existence of Dorothy O'Grady prior to the sensation of her arrest, trial and subsequent conviction in 1940 on charges of wartime treachery. Even fewer – possibly no one at all – were aware to any appreciable degree of her background. The small number of local residents she had, to an extent, befriended understood that she was not an islander by birth and had no apparent family links, past or present, with the island.

Possibly they knew that her husband, Vincent, had been a London County Council firefighter, not long retired after twenty-six years in the job, who had previously served with the Royal Navy, from whom he received a pension. They may have been aware that, at 42, Dorothy was nearly twenty years her husband's junior and that, shortly before the outbreak of war in 1939, the childless couple had moved from London to take over the running of Osborne Villa in Broadway, Sandown.

Located on the hilly southern fringe of the resort, directly opposite Sandown's military barracks, the guest house had advertised, before the couple's arrival, a combination of bed and breakfast and apartments as holiday accommodation 'two minutes from the sea'. A more accurate description would have been two minutes from the lofty cliff path overlooking the majestic sweep of Sandown Bay.

Some in the locality might also have known that, in a previous switch from the capital during the early 1930s, the O'Gradys had enjoyed an earlier spell of residence at Osborne Villa and had then moved the short distance to live at New Road in Lake, the village linking Sandown with Shanklin in the area of the bay, returning to London in 1938 before moving back to the Isle of Wight in 1939.

If the locals had previously been unaware of these facts, they would learn of most in 1940 when the press reported what they could of the court proceedings that led to Dorothy O'Grady's conviction and death sentence at the end of that dramatic year. The public, however, would be kept waiting for years before fuller details of her pre-war life became known. In 1940 she was largely an enigma.

From those newspaper reports it is clear just how detached Dorothy was from the local community. She was described in the island's press as 'a very reserved woman'. The principal newspaper, the *Isle of Wight County Press*, reported that 'even her next-door neighbour … did not know her name until the police called in the course of their enquiries'. Sandown's own paper, the *Isle of Wight Chronicle*, told how Dorothy was regarded by at least one resident as 'a person of dual personality, the more pronounced side being that of a child-like simplicity'.

Six decades after the war's end, Rene Old, who was working in Sandown at the time of O'Grady's arrest, remembered her as 'a cunning sort of a woman … she had a squeaky voice'. Betty Vine, who met Dorothy in later life, recalled a friend's description of her as 'cold and wet'. Indeed, a marked lack of warmth is apparent in reading, or speaking with people, about Dorothy O'Grady in wartime.

The couple's guest house enterprise at Osborne Villa had been short-lived, dramatically interrupted by the outbreak of war with Germany in September 1939. With no guests to accommodate, Dorothy soon lost the company of her husband too. As the perceived threat in London of aerial onslaught from the well-equipped Luftwaffe intensified, Vincent O'Grady responded to an appeal for ex-firefighters to return to service in the city, principally to help train the men of the newly formed Auxiliary Fire Service (AFS). With his departure,

Dorothy was left with only the companionship of her pet dog, a cross-bred black retriever named Rob – destined to play a key role in the dramatic events that followed.[1]

The affection Dorothy O'Grady felt for the family pet is clearly evident from the 1940 press reports of her trial. 'Mrs O'Grady had no converse with her neighbours,' the *Isle of Wight Chronicle* told its readers:

> but will be remembered as a short, dark little woman wearing rimmed spectacles who took her walks in the evening, apparently to exercise her dog … a woman friend who got to know her a little said that she thought more of her dog than of her husband and herself. She would even go without a meal to provide one for the animal.

It seems that those long walks with Rob were just as frequently taken during daytime – to one or other of the local beaches so that he could cool off in the sea – and it was Dorothy's fondness for these outings which first brought her into conflict with the military authorities. 'The island was full of soldiers and most of the seafront was prohibited to residents,' she would later tell a national newspaper. 'But the summer was hot and I continued to take my dog for his swim.'

From the available evidence it is clear that O'Grady's determination to ensure Rob had his bathe was a constant irritant to the army. She was repeatedly ushered away from the forbidden seashore. 'I walked miles to get the better of the soldiers in order to reach the beach,' she admitted in the first of her many press interviews following her release from prison in 1950. The soldiers' patience was tested to the limit until, on 9 August, it snapped. She was apprehended on the beach at Yaverland, close to the north-eastern tip of Sandown Bay beneath the high downs that culminate at Culver Cliff, which itself lies to the south of Bembridge, the most easterly of the Isle of Wight's villages.

A defensive bulwark guarding the eastern approach to the Solent, and handily placed to help protect the bay, this was a part of the island's coastline with particular military sensitivity. Culver Fire Command orchestrated a series of coastal artillery positions during the war, on or near the promontory after which it was named. Together, they made up a key part of Portsmouth's outer defences.

The batteries were well positioned and well armed. Nodes Fort, built at the start of the twentieth century at Nodes Point, St Helens, north-west of Culver, had been equipped by the onset of war with a combination of 9.2in and 6in guns – two of each. Much higher up, Culver Down Battery dated from 1906 and occupied a windswept site atop the Down, protected seaward by the virtually unclimbable Culver Cliff. It was equipped with a pair of 9.2in guns.

Firepower was not the only deterrent on Culver in 1940. For a short while in July the headland battery was also the experimental site for army-manned radar, located behind the guns. One of a type known as Chain Home Low (CHL), it was designed to detect shipping and aircraft flying below the height monitored by Chain Home (CH) stations such as RAF Ventnor on St Boniface Down. In August 1940, after the army radar's relocation to nearby Fort Bembridge, reserve equipment brought hastily to the Isle of Wight in the wake of the Luftwaffe's double strike on RAF Ventnor was located close to Culver on Bembridge Down. The mobile apparatus took over Ventnor's strategically vital role for two months from 23 August until the permanent station was returned to use.

Throughout the war, the Royal Navy operated a long-established shore signals and wireless station on Culver Down, constructed by the Marconi company in 1903.

To the south-west of the headland stood Yaverland's own batteries and, to the north-west, Fort Bembridge, the military sites closest to O'Grady when she defied the wartime regulations and strayed onto the shore that sunny August afternoon.

Whether or not she was aware that neither of the Yaverland batteries were functioning as heavy gun sites in 1940 remains a matter for conjecture. Yaverland Battery itself, within a fort dating from the 1860s, had been armed with a pair of 6in guns up until the mid-1930s (and would be again from 1943 until more than a decade after the war's conclusion) but the battery's immediate pre-war role had been that of an establishment for experimental artillery. In the summer of 1940 its sole, though still vitally important, contribution to the Culver area defences was as a location for coastal searchlights.

Some 1,000yd further east, right on the edge of the cliff from which it took its name, stood Redcliff Battery, another of the island's many 1860s defences built as part of the shield against perceived French naval aggression. Subject virtually from the start to coastal erosion, Redcliff had been abandoned before the turn of the century as a battery but was utilised in 1940 as an anti-aircraft gun post.[2]

Behind Yaverland and Redcliff, less than a mile away, Fort Bembridge occupied a commanding position high on Bembridge Down and was the Culver area's dominating military feature. A further relic of the nineteenth century, six-sided and surrounded by a deep, dry ditch, the fort provided barracks accommodation in 1940 for men operating the coastal artillery sites. It served too as the co-ordinating battery observation post and position finding cell for Culver Fire Command, also housing the army's radar facility after this was moved from Culver.[3]

The fact that, on the day she was arrested by the army, Dorothy O'Grady was also near to Sandown (Granite) Fort, close to the northern (Yaverland) end of Sandown's seafront parade – and had possibly walked past it on her way out of town – was of less significance. As was the case with Sandown Barracks Battery, virtually next door to her home at Osborne Villa, the decommissioned fort, dating from 1864, had not been reactivated for military use in the Second World War, though a newly built pill box emplacement sat prominently above its frontage. Whatever she knew of the weaponry and military establishments around Culver, Dorothy was in an area the army was very keen to keep civilians away from.[4, 5]

It was not only the wartime regulations that prohibited public access to the island's coast – there was usually the physical barrier of barbed wire to deter would-be trespassers. Neither had proved an obstacle to Dorothy O'Grady when soldiers approached her on 9 August. Among them was Lance-Corporal Bob McAlister, serving with the Royal Northumberland Fusiliers, who would much later provide a detailed account of the exchange which triggered the whole O'Grady saga – although he was not actually called to give evidence at her trial.

Having served with the ill-fated British Expeditionary Force in France, the Northumberland Fusiliers were now a constituent unit of the Isle of Wight's garrison force formed by men of the 12th Infantry Brigade, part of the army's 4th Division. Recently arrived on the island, the brigade's principal brief had been to equip the local coastline with the defensive capability to withstand, or at least hinder, any attempt at cross-Channel invasion by French-based German forces. The beach obstacles and other deterrents to a landing were their handiwork.[6]

If O'Grady's much later version of events is to be believed, she had been exercising her dog 'on Culver Cliff' (presumably a generalised reference to the Downs which end at the cliff-face) that August day when the retriever suddenly disappeared down a slope near Yaverland. Finding no barbed wire at that point to inhibit her progress, she had followed the animal down to the beach below. Having sat down to relax, read and eat an apple while Rob splashed contentedly in the waves, Dorothy was disturbed by the approach of the soldiers. 'They wanted to know what I was doing and said I was sitting beneath a hidden gun,' she would tell an *Isle of Wight Weekly Post* reporter in 1981.[7, 8, 9]

The 'hidden gun' did not feature when Bob McAlister recalled the incident for the *Isle of Wight County Press* in 1995. 'I had warned her twice before not to enter the zoned-off area,' he said. 'She always claimed she was looking for her dog and at first I believed her. But the more it happened, the more I became suspicious of her actions. I took her to the officer-in-charge, who handed her to the police.'

The former soldier, a 77-year-old Isle of Wight resident in Shanklin at the time of the press interview, did not recall O'Grady carrying anything that would suggest she had been engaged in some form of espionage and said she had not resisted in any way. However, he added, the tearful landlady did try to bribe her way out of trouble. 'She offered me ten bob [shillings] to let her go. It was a lot of money, as I was only on 14 bob a week, but I had no choice but to arrest her.'[10, 11]

O'Grady made no attempt when interviewed by the local press four decades after the event to hide the fact that she had attempted to hand over money following her military arrest on the beach – though she referred to soldiers in the plural rather than to Lance-Corporal McAlister alone. 'I felt I had caused them enough bother and offered them ten shillings for cigarettes. That was quite a lot of money for those days, so it made them suspicious,' she told the *Weekly Post*.

Rob the retriever was probably happier than his mistress when their walk was promptly extended. They were escorted for the better part of 3 miles along the roads around the foot of the Downs between Yaverland and Bembridge. 'I was reluctant to go with them to Bembridge, to the officer,' Dorothy recalled to the *Weekly Post* in 1981. 'It was a hot day and a long walk, but that probably made them even more suspicious. When we arrived, the officer kept asking me why I was offering bribes, but I told him I had not considered the money to be a bribe.'[12]

The soldiers may have refused to accept money from O'Grady, but, according to her account of the day's events, she was a willing recipient of the army's generosity at the end of the trek to Bembridge. After taking her name and address, the officer offered her a chocolate – then told his men to take her to the nearest bus stop, from where she travelled home to Osborne Villa. If the army did suspect that she had been up to no good, they had a rather odd way of showing it. Interestingly, irrespective of what his superior may have felt, Bob McAlister seems quickly to have made up his mind about O'Grady's guilt: 'After the arrest many local people damned us because they thought she was just a harmless crackpot,' he recalled, 'but we never really had any doubts about her.'

Evidently, news of the military arrest had spread quickly in the Sandown area, causing considerable excitement among the more impressionable sections of the local community. Peter Gattrell was a 12-year-old schoolboy living in Lake, a short downhill walk from O'Grady's home. He and his friends had picked up on the first whispers suggesting Dorothy might have been indulging in decidedly anti-patriotic activity on the beach. 'I walked past her house each morning and back again every night,' he recalled decades later:

My friends and I used to see her go in and out. At night we would listen at the door and we were sure we could hear morse code being tapped. We had little torches and shone them up at the windows. We used to think she was shining a light back at ours. There were bricked-up windows there. We were certain they hid secret doors!

Acting on the information they received from the military, the island's police issued two summonses against O'Grady, alleging offences under the Defence (General) Regulations of 1939. An officer called at Osborne Villa to deliver them. The first accused her of 'entering on the foreshore, contrary to regulation 16a', while the second alleged she had been 'acting in a manner likely to prevent or interfere with the performance of the duties of persons of HM Forces'. With O'Grady, despite her attempted use of financial inducement, apparently suspected by the police of being nothing more sinister than a wartime trespasser, needing to be taught a lesson, she was ordered to answer the charges before magistrates sitting as the County Bench at the Town Hall court in Ryde on 27 August. But when the case was called, there was no sign of her.[13]

The court adjourned for two hours to allow for the serving of a warrant forcing O'Grady's attendance. The two hours passed, but there was still no sign of her. The magistrates waited in vain for a further twenty minutes. They were told the police had been unable to execute the warrant. When officers called at Osborne Villa, they had found it locked and there had been no trace of the defendant. Pinned to the back door of the house was the message, 'No more milk till I return'.

The neighbours had no idea where she had gone, adding a degree of mystery and intrigue to the unfolding drama. The police were able to deduce only one thing – wherever Dorothy O'Grady had vanished to, she had taken her dog with her. Official perceptions immediately and understandably changed as the search for O'Grady covered the Isle of Wight and was then extended to the mainland, into various parts of southern England. For another two weeks, Dorothy evaded capture.

Naturally, during the course of their hunt, the police called one evening on Vincent O'Grady in London. An officer from Scotland Yard asked the clearly perplexed returnee firefighter if he knew of his wife's whereabouts. If she wasn't at Osborne Villa, said Mr O'Grady in reply, he had no idea where she was. The policeman, 'with commendable consideration and tact', according to the *Isle of Wight Chronicle*, then broke to him the news of his wife's arrest and subsequent disappearance. 'He had been wholly unaware that anything had occurred after leaving her behind in Sandown,' added the *Chronicle*. Vincent O'Grady convinced his enquiring visitor that he was as much in the dark as everybody else about his wife's vanishing act. It is clear his word was never doubted by the police.

He was left to concentrate as best he could on the dramatic new twist in the German aerial offensive against Britain – the bombing of its cities and, specifically, the start of what would turn out to be seventy-six consecutive nights of raids by the Luftwaffe on London. The mental state of Vincent O'Grady in early September 1940, as the Blitz was unleashed on the capital, can only be guessed at.

It would not have improved markedly with the news of his wife's recapture on 10 September. Leaving the island undetected would have been virtually impossible for Dorothy. It was hard enough for those with a legitimate reason to travel, such was the high level of security at that time. Instead, she had fled just about as far as anyone in the east of the Isle of Wight could have done that summer without catching a ferry – to the far west of the island. She was arrested by the police at a guest house in the village of Totland Bay, 2.5 miles short of The Needles, the western-most point, and 21 miles from Sandown.

Few facts relating to O'Grady's arrest in Totland were made public at the time. Again, several decades would pass before the full circumstances were finally revealed. Interviewed by the *Isle of Wight County Press* in 1995, Dennis Gould, by then aged 72 and living in East Cowes, recalled often seeing Dorothy in zoned-off coastal areas not far from Eden Road, Totland, his family home in 1940, during her weeks on the run. He remembered how she once asked him about the location of gun emplacements in the area. 'She tried to bribe me and my two cousins with money,' he said. 'She once gave us sixpence, which we spent on sweets, but obviously we did not pass on any information to her. We told our fathers and they told the police, who set up a surveillance operation.'[14]

Dennis Gould remembered that it was at Latton House, a still functioning guest house in Madeira Road, which runs from Totland's village centre the short distance to the area above the bay itself, that the police caught up with O'Grady. 'I was told officers had to knock a toilet door down to get at her,' he added, recalling that the arrest was made by PC William Drew and a Sergeant Taylor. Though Mr Gould did not refer to it, there are stories that the runaway landlady was actually attempting to flush documents down the toilet pan when the police burst in.

It would have been noted that, at Totland, O'Grady was again in close proximity to militarily sensitive locations, with a cluster of forts and batteries near to the village guarding the western approach, The Needles Passage, to the Solent.

Soon it would be no secret that, when recaptured, O'Grady was found to have been staying in the guest house under an assumed name. Escorted to the police station at the nearby town of Yarmouth, she was naturally asked why she had not turned up for her court hearing in Ryde. 'I was too scared to attend,' she replied.

Now in custody, she was taken the next day to her home town police station at Sandown for a brief appearance before two magistrates at a specially convened occasional court. Unsurprisingly, given her disappearing act, the police had prepared an application that, if granted, would keep her under lock and key pending further enquiries. For the moment, the holding charge was that, on 9 August, the day of her initial arrest at Yaverland, she 'unlawfully did a certain act having reasonable cause to believe that it would be likely to prevent or interfere with the performance of the duties of persons of His Majesty's Services, or the carrying on of their work in the performance of essential services'.

This ambiguously worded accusation – did it now imply a specific act in breach of the Defence Regulations over and above unlawful presence? – was augmented by the police making clear to the magistrates that it was 'quite likely' other charges would be preferred and that the case would be taken up by the Director of Public Prosecutions. Clearly, this was now a serious matter. What had the police discovered? Quite a lot, it would eventually transpire – and they hadn't had to search very hard to find it, either – but the evidence that had brought Dorothy O'Grady back to Sandown under police escort was reserved for the ears of those who needed to know – and that did not include the special court.

The police successfully applied for O'Grady to be remanded in custody until 1 October. The milkman would have no need to call at Osborne Villa for some time. Dorothy O'Grady left Sandown behind, bound for London's Holloway prison.

## Notes

1   The Auxiliary Fire Service (AFS) was formed in January 1938 to supplement the work of local authority fire brigades in the event of war. In August 1941 the AFS and the local brigades were replaced for the remainder of the war – and up until 1948 – by the newly formed National Fire Service (NFS).

2   Remains of the former batteries survive today at Nodes Fort and Yaverland Fort – both within holiday complexes – and on Culver Down, where the former 9.2in gun emplacements are available for public inspection in the care of the National Trust. All three had remained in military use until the dissolution of the British Army's Coast Artillery in 1956. Virtually nothing has survived of Redcliff Battery.

3   Fort Bembridge's military function ended with the cessation of hostilities in 1945. Formally relinquished by the army in 1948, the fort remains intact, partly occupied by a light engineering tenant of the National Trust. Volunteers have been clearing the largely derelict remainder to permit guided tours.

4   Although Sandown Barracks Battery, alongside O'Grady's Osborne Villa home, had been discarded by the military before the Second World War, the barracks themselves – opposite the O'Grady house – were still in use.

5 The wartime pill box is still evident today, now guarding the frontage of what has become the Isle of Wight Zoo.

6 It is still possible to see remains of the Isle of Wight's wartime anti-invasion measures – notably, several coastal gun emplacements and the 'dragon's teeth' obstacles which survive on the shore at Bembridge.

7 If O'Grady had been exercising her dog anywhere near Culver Cliff, as she claimed, she would already have been in breach of the regulations. The cliff and adjacent Downs were officially barred to the public.

8 If there was a 'hidden gun' it was presumably the weapon at Redcliff Battery's anti-aircraft position. It seems a strange piece of information for the army to share with a civilian who had wandered off limits.

9 In her account of the military arrest when she was interviewed in 1950 by the *Sunday Express*, O'Grady referred to the location as Whitecliff Bay, which lies close to Bembridge on the north-facing shore of Culver – i.e. 'round the corner' of the promontory from Yaverland, the far more likely location. This is not supported by the available evidence, though the disappearance in 2006 from The National Archives of the prosecution's trial papers has naturally hindered any prospect of cross-checking the facts.

10 O'Grady's trial papers, made public in 1995, included a statement from Private James McNally, who was with McAlister when Dorothy was apprehended on the beach, suggesting that it was he who was offered the 10s bribe. The probability is that the attempted inducement was aimed at both soldiers. Other reports suggest it was men from the 6th Black Watch – another constituent unit of 12th Brigade in the summer of 1940 – who were involved in the military arrest. Neither of these points can now be checked for accuracy owing to the 'loss' of the trial records at The National Archives – see Chapter 11.

11 10s (ten bob) was half of £1. Thus it equates to 50p in modern decimal currency but would have had the purchasing power of somewhere between £20 and £22.50 in Britain today.

12 O'Grady's interview with the officer probably occurred at Bembridge School, taken over by the army in the summer of 1940 after its staff and pupils had moved for the war's duration to the Lake District.

13 The island was policed in 1940 by the Isle of Wight County Constabulary. It is now under the jurisdiction of the Hampshire Constabulary.

14 Sixpence was half of 1s. It equates to 2.5p in modern currency but would have had the purchasing power of around £1 today.

# 4

# ON EVIDENCE THAT ADMITTED NO DOUBT

Speculation was mounting in the Isle of Wight. Hard facts were scarce, but the gossip was fed by all manner of theories and statements claimed as fact – though mostly in the hushed tones which paid lip service to the Ministry of Information's warning, first issued in February 1940, that 'careless talk costs lives'. The strange events surrounding the disappearance from their midst of Dorothy O'Grady were a novel distraction for islanders from the bombs – and stricken aircraft of both sides – that were raining down on their offshore homeland.

Had there really been a spy living among them, as many were now keen to assert? Local newspapers were scanned regularly for the answer. The island's press had reported briefly on O'Grady's failure to answer the charges against her at Ryde in August and, a fortnight later, her appearance before the court in Sandown, but it wasn't until the first week of October that they could write the next chapter in the story of the rather odd seaside landlady's apparent misdeeds. Dorothy had finally made her delayed appearance before the magistrates at Ryde on Tuesday 1 October, as scheduled by the earlier hearing in her home town. The police had sought to extend her remand in prison by a further fourteen days.

It was front page news in the *Isle of Wight Chronicle*. The report confirmed for readers that the allegations concerned breaches of the Defence Regulations and added that the superintendent making the remand application felt justified in doing so as the matter was in the hands of the Director of Public Prosecutions and he understood 'other charges would be preferred'. On the face of it, the legal situation was exactly as it had been at the court in Sandown three weeks earlier.

The application was not contested by O'Grady's solicitor, H.R. Palmer, but, reported the *Chronicle*, the Newport-based lawyer did seek an assurance from the Chairman of the Bench, Sir Godfrey Baring, that 'facilities would be afforded for medical oversight' to be kept on his client. Was this a reference to O'Grady's physical or mental state? Mr Palmer, from the long-established Roach Pittis practice, did not elucidate but Sir Godfrey duly assured him that 'the customary facilities of that nature would be available' to the accused. As Vincent O'Grady looked on from the public gallery, the eight magistrates making up the Bench granted the application. Dorothy O'Grady was returned to jail.

The fortnight that passed before her reappearance at the court in Ryde was a period of relative calm in the Isle of Wight's war, thus providing ample opportunity for local speculation on the precise nature of the crime – that 'certain act' that had contravened the wartime regulations – perpetrated by the landlady of Osborne Villa; the unknown extent and composition of the DPP's expected further charges; and the possible outcome of O'Grady's next appointment at the town hall. Some of the circulating local gossip was better-informed than most.

Working in civil defence as a young dispatch rider in the West Wight, Vera Woodhead had been alerted to a particularly strong rumour. 'We were told that someone had been cutting wires up through the roads to Alum Bay,' she recalled nearly seventy years later. Alum Bay is tucked into the coastline immediately north-east of The Needles – just below the twin batteries (Needles Old and Needles New) that dominated the headland leading to the famous chalk stacks. 'We didn't know who it was at first, but then they discovered this woman at Totland,' the former dispatch rider – now Vera Callaway – added in 2010.

In Sandown, as the day of O'Grady's return to court drew closer, some of the few people who had come into contact with her prior to her initial arrest reflected on Dorothy's surprising openness about her visits to the zoned-off beach areas. 'We were going to Bembridge,' recalled Rene Old. 'She said – "I've been down there, down on the beach." She assured us we could do that, too!'

Many thought there had to have been a mistake. Dorothy O'Grady was an odd woman, but realistically she couldn't be a spy – could she? The locals were curious, yet doubtful, some dismissive, of the possibility that Dorothy had been working for the enemy. She had done something wrong, no doubt, but it would surely turn out to be nothing more sinister than silliness. She wasn't a spy. There again, what did a spy look like? And what about the infamous fifth column? They waited for it all to be clarified – and were astounded when it was.

On Tuesday 15 October, the town hall courtroom at Ryde was filled for O'Grady's reappearance before the magistrates. Transported back to the Isle of Wight from Holloway the previous morning, she had spent the time since in the cells at Ryde police station. Many years later, it would be revealed how remarkably talkative she had been during what turned out to be a two-night stay with the local police, but she was to say very little when she arrived at court on the Tuesday morning for the start of a hearing that would last one-and-a-half days and end with her committal to a higher court for trial by judge and jury.

The seriousness of O'Grady's situation was obvious by the time she left the town hall on the Wednesday. To the original charges under the Defence Regulations – entering on the foreshore and acting in a manner likely to interfere with the forces – had been added a raft of new allegations under the same emergency legislation, to make a total of eight counts. The charge sheet now showed clearly that the DPP – and the MI5 officers who had interviewed O'Grady in Holloway prior to the court hearing – were persuaded that she really had been involved in espionage activity on the Isle of Wight for the Third Reich. Yet, there was little in the way of detail emerging from the press reports that week to satisfy the public's curiosity. Indeed, most of the facts behind the charges were destined to remain matters for public conjecture for more than half a century.

G.R. Paling, for the DPP, had set the long train of secrecy in motion at the Ryde committal with an application to the Bench under the provisions of the Emergency Powers Act 1939. The magistrates, he said, had the power to order that the proceedings should take place in camera – with the press and public excluded – as the evidence was such that a closed court 'would be expedient in the interests of public safety'. There was no objection to this from the defence, leaving the chairman, Sir Godfrey Baring, and his six fellow magistrates with an easy decision to make. The court was cleared of all except witnesses and officials.

This restricted press coverage, and thus the public's understanding, of O'Grady's committal to the minimum. The evidence used to commit her for trial was not available for public consumption. Neither were the identities of the witnesses. But, while the wording of the charges – read in open court – was all there was to feed the public appetite for information, it was at least a tasty morsel.

Lining up beneath the two initial charges, three separate counts now seemed to refer to the alleged 'certain act' that had first been mentioned at the occasional court in Sandown on 11 September. One of these, effectively the holding charge used at Sandown, claimed that, with intent to help the enemy, O'Grady had unlawfully carried out the unspecified act which, said the prosecution, had been 'designed or likely' to impede the nation's 'naval, military or air operations'.

Another, subtly different, charge alleged the act in question had been likely to assist the enemy, while the third added a new twist – that, with intent to help the enemy, O'Grady had unlawfully conspired with another, unknown, to commit the act. It was all a bit vague. Had there been more than one specific act? And more than one spy? Just who had Dorothy O'Grady been conspiring with?

The wording of the three remaining charges threw rather more light on the precise nature of the crimes allegedly committed by the

Sandown landlady. She was accused that, 'for a purpose prejudicial to the safety or interest of the State', she had unlawfully made a plan, 'calculated to be, or which might be, or was intended to be, directly or indirectly useful to the enemy'. The prosecution additionally claimed that she had attempted to force a safeguard (in effect, she'd tried to break through the military measures in place to protect an area) and had acted with intent to impede the work of 'certain apparatus' used by the military.

O'Grady spoke only to confirm her full name, Dorothy Pamela O'Grady, her age, 42, her home address at Osborne Villa and her status, prior to arrest, as a housewife. Committed to stand trial at the Hampshire Assizes in Winchester (there being no court of equivalent level on the Isle of Wight), she was returned to prison.

No doubt, once back there, her legal representatives set out for her the extreme seriousness of her situation. The composition of the charges was such that, if convicted, she faced the very real prospect of a very long term of imprisonment – theoretically for life. Should the prosecution prove that she actually had forced a military safeguard, recent amendments to the Defence Regulations provided a new penalty. Forcing safeguards had become a capital offence. There was now a chance that, when Dorothy O'Grady stood trial, her life might be at stake – and the shadow of the gallows would shortly move menacingly closer.

Just over a week before Christmas 1940, on Monday 16 December, O'Grady travelled from Holloway in the company of prison officers to face the might of English wartime justice at the nation's ancient capital in Hampshire. Presiding over her fate in the courtroom at Winchester Castle's medieval Great Hall was Mr Justice Macnaghten, an Ulsterman knighted in 1920 as Sir Malcolm Macnaghten, who had sat as a High Court judge since 1928. Thus the stage was set for two people with Gaelic surnames, but very little else in common, to take the starring roles in what was now emerging as a sensational British drama.[1,2]

Suitably imposing in wig and gown, a month short of his seventy-second birthday, Macnaghten faced an unlikely defendant who, reported the *Daily Mirror* under the front page headlines the following day, was 'short, dark, bespectacled … dressed neatly but plainly in a green overcoat with a heavy fur collar'. Fleet Street was there in force, intrigued and then evidently bewildered by the look and demeanour of the defendant who, said the *Mirror*, 'stood calmly in the dock between two women warders'. The tabloid's obviously fascinated court reporter added: 'Her glasses gave her almost a benign appearance – unlike a woman who would betray her country … when the trial began she looked light-hearted.'

Noting somewhat esoterically that O'Grady was standing on 'practically the same spot' occupied by Alice Lisle, sentenced to death by the notorious Judge Jeffreys in 1685 for her treachery in harbouring rebels in the wake of the Monmouth Rebellion, the *Daily Telegraph*'s choice of adjective was 'unperturbed'.[3]

Collectively, the journalists in the courtroom could have been forgiven for wondering – was Dorothy O'Grady enjoying herself? It was a question that would be repeated many times in the years that followed. However, it seems her apparent good cheer in the Winchester dock did not last. 'In the brief time the public remained in court she took the proceedings seriously,' added the *Daily Mirror*.

As well she might. The DPP had re-framed the charge sheet, which now ran to nine counts and represented a threat to O'Grady even more ominous than it had appeared at her committal. While she was still accused of breaching the wartime Defence Regulations several times over, the bespectacled 42-year-old former landlady now faced allegations brought under two further Acts of Parliament – the Official Secrets Act of 1911 and the new Treachery Act, which had entered the statute book only seven months before the O'Grady trial (see Chapter 1) and which had been utilised to frame the first three charges against her.

Respectively, counts one, two and three related to the allegation of conspiracy with intent to help the enemy; making a plan likely to assist the enemy's military operations; and, with intent to impede the British armed forces, cutting a military telephone wire. These three charges were upgraded from the list of allegations under the Defence Regulations which had been used at the Ryde committal. This upgrading was of immense significance. All three charges, if proven, would now be capital offences. The penalty for conviction on any one of these allegations was automatic under the terms of the 1940 Treachery Act – death.

If they couldn't get her on this trio of 'headline' charges, the prosecution could pin their hopes on the Defence Regulations to secure a capital conviction with count four – which now alleged she had actually forced, rather than merely attempted to force, a military safeguard. If this also failed to produce the desired result, a successful outcome with count five alone, brought under the Official Secrets Act, alleging that, for purposes prejudicial to the State, she had approached a prohibited place, would leave O'Grady facing up to fourteen years in prison.

And there were still four other charges in the Crown's armoury. With counts six and seven, the DPP also accused O'Grady under the Official Secrets Act with making a plan of potential use to the enemy, an act which might prove prejudicial to the nation's defence. Counts eight and nine, under the Defence Regulations, respectively alleged sabotage (cutting the telephone wire) and the possession of a document (the plan referred to in other charges) with information purporting to relate to the nation's defensive measures. Clearly, the Crown was determined to nail Dorothy O'Grady as an enemy spy – one way or another.

Represented in court by barrister John Scott Henderson, O'Grady had entered not guilty pleas to all nine charges before, inevitably, the court was cleared of public and press for the presentation of the evidence in camera, in response to an application from the prosecution team, led by John Trapnell KC. A trial of such a sensitive nature in wartime Britain was always destined to be held in secret.[4]

The trial continued in closed session for the best part of two days until the jury had heard the evidence from what had obviously been a lengthy string of witnesses (including, reporters noted, MI5 officers), listened to the closing arguments from counsel and the judge's summing-up, and then retired to consider the validity of the prosecution's case. There were many who missed the trial's finale, caught on the hop by the jury's quicker than expected return. 'Reporters and a few jurymen waiting for the next case alone saw the final scene,' the *Daily Express* revealed the next day. They witnessed a dramatic conclusion.

Dorothy O'Grady had been partially successful in her blanket denial of all nine charges. On counts one (conspiracy) and four (forcing a safeguard) she had been found not guilty. It hardly mattered. The jury returned guilty verdicts on all seven remaining charges. Mr Justice Macnaghten passed no sentences on counts five to nine. There was no need when the only penalty for conviction on counts two and three, making the plan and cutting the military telephone wire – both in contravention of the Treachery Act – rendered any further sentencing pointless.

Did she have anything to say before sentencing? Dorothy O'Grady was asked. She shook her head. 'In the growing darkness in the Great Hall of Winchester Castle, the judge donned the black cap,' reported the *Isle of Wight Chronicle* in a dramatic account of what was almost certainly its biggest-ever local news story. The Sandown housewife stood in the dock expressionless, giving no visible sign that she was aware of, or concerned by, the ominous significance of the small square of black cloth as it was solemnly positioned on the judge's head, 'amidst an impressive silence', according to the *Isle of Wight County Press*'s own report of the tense drama. As Mr Justice Macnaghten pronounced sentence, reported the *Daily Mirror*, O'Grady 'listened, unmoved'. She confronted the judge 'sullenly, with mask-like face', the *Daily Express* told its readers.

Gravely, he told her, 'On evidence that admitted no doubt, the jury have found you guilty of treachery. For that crime the law prescribes but one sentence and it is my duty to pass that sentence upon you.' Dorothy O'Grady continued to listen in silence as Macnaghten pronounced the inevitable sentence of death by hanging.

What was going through her mind? O'Grady would eventually provide the answer to this, an answer that would not have occurred to anyone in the Great Hall at Winchester that December day in 1940.

But for the moment, she was keeping her thoughts to herself. 'When the judge had finished speaking,' recorded the *Isle of Wight Chronicle*, 'she walked firmly from the dock without breaking the silence which had fallen in the tense case. To the last she presented just the same calmness, almost sullen indifference, as had marked her several appearances before the Isle of Wight County Magistrates in the court at Ryde.'

It was easier for the journalists to gauge the emotions of Vincent O'Grady – said in contemporary reports to have been 'dismayed and astonished when he heard of the charges against his wife' – as he watched her depart the courtroom without glancing at him late on that Tuesday afternoon. 'Under very trying circumstances,' the *Chronicle* added in its account the next day:

> Mr O'Grady has made a gallant attempt to continue his work in London, but the nerve-racking experience in the air raids, combined with the natural worry regarding his wife, has proved too much and he has resigned. Last night he was at home at Osborne Villa and with him was his sister, who is also looking after the retriever dog.

It must have seemed a sadly ironic, desperately tragic, situation for Dorothy's husband, who, the local press noted sympathetically, had 'brought his wife to Sandown shortly before the war with the idea of settling down in quiet retirement'.

After the trial's climax, Vincent remained as mystified about his wife's criminal activity as he had been when the news of her arrest was first broken to him in London. 'Since legal proceedings were instigated, his wife has been very reluctant to see him,' the *Chronicle* reported. 'He had a few words with her following her committal by the Island magistrates but she refused to see him when she was on remand at Holloway prison and wrote asking him not to visit her there.'

Vincent O'Grady might not have been able to speak with his wife, but he could certainly read about her. The headlines in the local and, especially, the national press ('BETRAYED BRITAIN – HOUSEWIFE TO DIE' thundered the *Daily Mirror*'s front page splash on 18 December) must have made particularly uncomfortable reading for Dorothy's troubled husband as the story of her conviction spread around the country. Her death sentence was such a sensational story, the *Mirror* elected to lead on it ahead of the massively significant announcement of US plans to pour a huge amount of arms and ammunition into Britain on loan – proposals that would soon evolve into the lend-lease arrangement crucial to Britain's ability to carry on the fight against Hitler.

What, if anything, had Dorothy O'Grady told the court in her defence? What had *been* her defence? What had she included on her infamous plan? What had the witnesses said? And the respective counsel in their closing speeches? What points of law had the judge brought to the jury's attention in his summing-up? And how on earth had this admittedly odd but otherwise outwardly unremarkable woman become an active Nazi agent as her convictions firmly implied? It would be years, decades in some cases, before the answers to these key questions were revealed. This was a story still very much in skeletal form in the wake of the Winchester trial, but the fact that O'Grady was now facing execution was meaty enough to turn it very quickly into an international news item.

As the first Briton (and destined to be the only woman) convicted of treachery under the 1940 Act, her imprint on the nation's historical record of notoriety was more than sufficient to secure her trial's inclusion in the widely read weekly digest of world events, *Keesing's Contemporary Archives*. Summarising a report in the *Daily Telegraph*, it coupled the news of O'Grady's death sentence with that of the hanging on 17 December of Dutchman Charles van den Kieboom, an enemy agent who had been found guilty under the Treachery Act with two other men after the trio were arrested soon after their arrival in a rowing boat on the Kent coast in September. Their executions were the first carried out under the Act. O'Grady and Van den Kieboom had more than their treachery convictions in common. Both had been condemned to die for working covertly in the interests of Nazi Germany without holding German citizenship.[5, 6]

O'Grady's nationality was naturally a matter of some interest in the wake of her trial. Was she of Irish descent? Might that help to explain the apparent sympathy for Germany which, it seemed, would soon claim her life? The press dug out the facts. 'It is as well we should add that Mrs O'Grady is not of Irish extraction, nor yet is she a Roman Catholic,' the *Isle of Wight Chronicle* reported. 'Further, she is in no way related to Dr Standish O'Grady and his widow mother, who also happen to reside in the Broadway, Sandown.' Despite this correctly being made clear at the time, the suggestion that Dorothy was an Irishwoman married to Dr O'Grady persists in some quarters to this day. In fact, as the *Chronicle* diligently pointed out, 'Mrs O'Grady is reported to be a Londoner by birth, the daughter of an employee of the British Museum annexe at Hendon.' It would eventually transpire that Dorothy's origins were not quite as straightforward as this, but in essence the Sandown newspaper had got it right.

On Wednesday 18 December, the day after her trial's dramatic conclusion, O'Grady's reception at Holloway as a condemned prisoner was formalised. She was escorted to the prison's condemned suite on the first floor – a wardrobe hiding the door to an empty room between the day cell and the execution chamber – where she was to spend Christmas and the New Year pending her scheduled appointment with the hangman. The Home Office had announced that it would take place on Tuesday 7 January 1941, just three weeks after the trial.

It is not clear which of Britain's most experienced trio of executioners at that time – Stanley Cross, Tom Pierrepoint or Tom Phillips – was put on stand-by to carry out the task, but archived records clearly name the man picked from the Home Office's approved list to act as his number two. Harry Allen, aged 29, had witnessed only one hanging, on 29 November, and his selection as assistant for Dorothy O'Grady's execution was actually the first formal appointment for the man who would eventually retire in 1964 as one of Britain's last two chief executioners.[7]

In Sandown on 19 December Vincent O'Grady received a visit from a *Daily Express* reporter keen to secure the inside story on the spying sensation that had gripped the nation. The outcome of their discussion was featured prominently in the *Express* the next morning. Vincent had clearly needed to talk. It was a poignant story.

The *Express* man opened his account by telling how, earlier that Thursday, Dorothy's husband had taken her black retriever dog to the vet to have him put to sleep. Rob, the much-loved pet who inadvertently had played such a significant part in Dorothy's demise, had been unable to cope with his mistress' continuing absence since her re-arrest in September. 'The dog has been pining so much ... that it was a mercy to have him put away,' the journalist wrote. It served as sadly symbolic of the traumatic collapse, within a period of less than sixteen months, in the fortunes of the O'Grady household – but Vincent had not yet reached the point of despair. 'The home ... he means to keep going, hoping that one day his wife will come back to it,' added the report.

Vincent had told his interviewer, 'We have had fifteen years of happiness together. I don't want to let her down now.' It was evident that, by his actions, he felt he had already contributed to Dorothy's now perilous situation. 'If I had thought more of my wife and less of my country, none of this would have happened,' he told the *Express*. 'I swear she was not in her right mind when she did it.'

The tears had 'welled' in Vincent O'Grady's eyes as he explained how, just before the war started, he had been contacted by his former fire brigade chief in London with the request for him to return to the service as a reservist. On 1 September 1939, two days before war was declared, added Vincent:

> I packed my suitcase, went back to London and reported for duty at my old station, Whitechapel. Like many old hands I thought London would be bombed right away. I knew that was where my country needed me. Now I know it was a fatal mistake. Had I stayed at home, everything would have been all right. She would have been here today with the housework, the cooking and me to look after. I had a good pension. But I left her all on her own, with only her dog as company.[8]

While in London, he revealed, he had received a disturbing letter from his wife following her disappearance in August, about which he had known nothing:

> It was a rambling sort of note. She spoke of being in a spot of bother, asked me to forgive her for bringing disgrace and trouble. 'Goodbye, all my love,' it ended. I was dumbfounded. Hadn't the slightest idea what the trouble was or where she was to be found. I even asked the Salvation Army to help find her.

Vincent continued:

> It is my 62nd birthday on Saturday. What a birthday! … But she must have been mad. I am praying that the sentence will be commuted and that, after the war, there will be an amnesty. She was such a good wife. I should never have gone away. I'm glad everything has been found out, but it's …

He left the sentence unfinished, adding only, 'Ah, she must have been mad.'[9, 10]

Vincent O'Grady had laid bare his feelings and evident bemusement at his wife's summer escapades. However, his depiction of the 'good wife' who had given him fifteen years of marital happiness, but had inexplicably strayed insanely out of character during his absence, was, for entirely understandable reasons, something of a rose-tinted assessment of Dorothy, as events years later would reveal.

## Notes

1    Famous as the venue for the so-called Bloody Assizes in the late seventeenth century – in the aftermath of the Battle of Sedgemoor which ended the Monmouth Rebellion in England – Winchester's Great Hall, restored in the 1870s, had resumed its role as a courtroom, after a long gap, in 1938. It was last used as such in 1974.

2  The fourth son of Lord Macnaghten Bt., Sir Malcolm Macnaghten (1869–1955) was educated at Eton and Trinity College, Cambridge, beginning a long legal career in 1894 when he became a barrister. His period as a High Court judge extended from 1928 to 1947. Macnaghten was also a politician, representing constituencies in County Londonderry as a Unionist MP between 1922 and 1929.

3  Lady Alice Lisle (1617–85) was tried by Jeffreys at the opening of the Bloody Assizes for sheltering a rebel fugitive, John Hickes, at her Moyles Court home near the Hampshire town of Ringwood. While she was not charged with harbouring a second rebel, the fact that she had done so helped to convict her.

4  J.G. Trapnell KC was a prominent English barrister in the 1930s and 1940s who also worked as a judge. At the time of Dorothy O'Grady's trial he was Judge Advocate of the Fleet, supervising the court-martial system in the Royal Navy, a post he held between 1933 and 1943. John Trapnell also served the English judiciary as Recorder of Plymouth and was the father of eminent scientific explorer Colin Trapnell.

5  The reference to Dorothy O'Grady's conviction as the first woman sentenced to death under the Treachery Act was published on 19 December 1940 in *Keesing's Contemporary Archive of World Events*.

6  Charles van den Kieboom (26) had been convicted with Carl Meier (24) and Jose Waldberg (22) at the Old Bailey on 22 November 1940. He was hanged at Pentonville one week after the other two agents.

7  Stanley Cross, who was on the Home Office list of executioners between 1932 and 1941, had executed Carl Meier and Jose Waldberg on 10 December 1940 (see footnote six). Harry Allen, on the list from 1941 to 1964, shared the chief executioner's role with Steve Wade following the 1956 resignation of Albert Pierrepoint, Tom Pierrepoint's nephew and Britain's most prolific twentieth-century hangman.

8  The call for Vincent O'Grady to return to firefighting duties had come from the top – from the felicitously named Commander Aylmer Newton George Firebrace, chief officer of the London Fire Brigade itself. Firebrace (1886–1972) had gained the rank of commander from his earlier service in the Royal Navy.

9  The letter Vincent O'Grady received in London from his wife presumably arrived after the police had called to inform him of Dorothy's arrest and subsequent disappearance – the first he knew of it. See Chapter 3.

10 See Chapter 7 for clarification of Vincent O'Grady's age.

# 5

# THE BULBS I PLANTED WILL COME UP AGAIN

With just three weeks in which to save her life, Dorothy O'Grady's legal team had to move fast. Access to legal aid, which would not be uniformly available in the UK until 1949, had earlier been secured to help fund her defence. It would now be used in the preparation of an appeal to halt the impending execution.[1]

In 45-year-old barrister John Scott Henderson, O'Grady had a bright lawyer destined for an illustrious career at the bar that would see him appointed Recorder of Portsmouth as a QC and chair high-profile government inquiries into fox hunting (1949) and the controversial execution of Timothy Evans for the alleged murders of his wife and daughter (1953). Decades later it would be revealed that in December 1940 he faced something of an uphill task to keep Dorothy O'Grady from the gallows in the face of high-lever insistence that she should hang, such were the jittery sensitivities of the British judiciary in wartime.[2]

On Boxing Day the defence made their move, giving formal notice of O'Grady's intention to appeal. This was not merely an entreaty against the death sentence handed down by the trial judge. Scott Henderson had framed an appeal against her actual conviction on the two capital charges – the guilty verdicts returned on counts two and three. In his view, Sir Malcolm Macnaghten's summing-up of the case for the Winchester jury had unfairly prejudiced the outcome. The evidence, Scott Henderson would argue, *had* admitted doubt as to O'Grady's intentions in doing what she clearly had done but the judge had, in effect, ignored this by conflating the capital and non-capital offences. Dorothy's ground for lodging the appeal would be on a points of law – misdirection of the jury.

This was enough to earn her a reprieve from the hangman. Formal leave to appeal was granted and the hearing before the Court of Criminal Appeal was set for London's Central Criminal Court (the Old Bailey) on Monday 10 February 1941. It would be heard by a very prominent trio of judges under Lord Caldecote – Sir Thomas Inskip – whose elevation to the peerage at the outbreak of war in 1939 had been followed in 1940 by his appointment as Lord Chief Justice. Caldecote would sit with Mr Justice Humphreys and Mr Justice Tucker.[3, 4]

It was entirely in keeping with the bizarre nature of Dorothy O'Grady's wartime story that the period preceding her Old Bailey appointment was marked with an unlikely new twist. By a strange quirk of fate her appeal was threatened with disarray thanks to a dramatic intervention by the enemy in whose interests she stood convicted of treachery. On 22 January 1941 the Luftwaffe scored a direct hit on John Scott Henderson's London chambers during a bombing raid on the capital, badly damaging the premises. The documents he was relying upon to support his legal arguments were totally destroyed. While this was an unhelpful act on the part of Dorothy's supposed wartime employers, it was manna from heaven for the conspiracy theorists, who no doubt convinced themselves (as some still do) that Nazi Germany was out to cover its tracks by eliminating potentially sensitive information with an early demonstration of precision bombing.

Equality was restored when Scott Henderson managed to win the co-operation of John Trapnell, who had led for the prosecution at Winchester and would be appearing for the Crown at the February appeal hearing. O'Grady's counsel moved temporarily into Trapnell's chambers where he was able to share the Crown's documents in preparing the ground to save Dorothy's life. Press reports of this quirky bombing incident added that the two barristers would 'take turns in using them' when the appeal was heard. The Luftwaffe had been thwarted!

If Dorothy O'Grady was fearful of the outcome at the Old Bailey hearing she betrayed no sign of it after arriving by car under prison escort. 'She seemed unperturbed as she entered the brass-railed dock,' reported the *Isle of Wight Chronicle*. 'She glanced first at the three judges, then at her husband, sitting along in the public seats, before taking her seat between two wardresses.' Dressed in the same green coat with heavy fur collar she had worn at Winchester, Dorothy had decided to top it off this time with a maroon hat, trimmed with ribbons of what the press could only describe as 'a lighter colour'. If her courtroom attire was perhaps a little loud, she countered it by answering her name in what reporters, desperate for detail, called 'a quiet, steady voice'.

For the Crown, John Trapnell immediately, and unsurprisingly, asked for the appeal, in line with the court hearings that had preceded it, to be held in secret, with press and public excluded from hearing the legal arguments. 'Appellant's counsel, Mr Scott Henderson, has informed me,' he said, 'that he intends only to raise points of law, but I am instructed to ask that the appeal be heard in camera in case it should be necessary to go into the facts. It is a matter of precaution.'

Although Lord Caldecote granted the request, the courtroom was not entirely cleared of the public. Vincent O'Grady was permitted to remain when an application by the defence for him to do so was approved. There was a condition. He was allowed to stay only after giving an undertaking that he would reveal nothing of the hearing. Vincent, to his credit, never betrayed that vow.

With the courtroom stage otherwise cleared of all but its essential characters, the legal arguments for and against Dorothy O'Grady's appeal continued for five hours, either side of a forty-five-minute break for lunch, which Dorothy spent in the cells. Then the public and press were readmitted to hear Lord Caldecote deliver in open court the outcome of the bid to save the Sandown housewife's life. The Lord Chief Justice wasted no time on preliminaries. He was straight to the point.

'The conviction on the two capital charges under the Treachery Act has been quashed,' he said, barely pausing long enough for the implication of his words to sink in. Dorothy O'Grady would not be keeping her appointment with the hangman.

But neither was she about to be set free. There was still the matter of the five other guilty verdicts handed down by the jury at the October trial. 'Sentence has been passed by the court on charges on which the appellant was convicted but on which the judge passed no sentence,' added Caldecote. 'This court has passed a sentence of 14 years' penal servitude on the counts other than those under the Treachery Act.' With the judgment delivered, Dorothy O'Grady, still apparently emotionless, was led from the dock, out of the court, and taken downstairs.

In a somewhat poignant post-script, her grey-haired husband picked up the small suitcase in which he had brought papers relating to the case and hurried from the courtroom 'I must go to my wife,' he told reporters. The couple were together for half-an-hour in the prisoners' quarters. Afterwards, he said: 'It is a great relief that the original sentence no longer stands, but 14 years is a very long time. I hope we shall meet again after the war, I shall keep a home for her to come to.'

Again, it was the *Daily Express* who secured the best of the interviews with Dorothy's husband, published the next day. More than once Vincent O'Grady referred to the fourteen-year sentence, his grief at the impending lengthy separation from his wife obvious, but he was, of course, able to look on the bright side. It could have been much worse. 'After her trial they branded her a traitor,' he said. 'She is free of that stigma today, thank God. A great weight is lifted off my mind now ...'

The report turned to the O'Gradys' thirty minutes together while the prison car waited outside the court to take Dorothy away. 'With the two wardresses sitting a little way from them, cups of tea before them, they talked and wept. Then one of the wardresses tapped the plump, bespectacled little woman on the shoulder. "I'm sorry – time to go," she whispered.' The couple's last words to each other were evidently overheard by the *Express* reporter, who recounted the exchange verbatim.

'Well Vin, this is the last time you'll kiss me. Promise me one thing –
don't let anyone else have my dog. I'd rather you had Rob put to sleep.
It would make me happy if you did,' murmured Dorothy.

'That's all right, my girl – it shall be done,' Vincent answered, not
revealing to his wife that her beloved pet had already been put out of its
misery. He had clearly made the right decision. Later, after Dorothy had
been driven away, he told the *Express*, 'She had left her meat coupons
with the butcher so that her dog might have his meals.' It seemed that
when Dorothy had left Osborne Villa for Totland Bay five months
earlier, she had not expected to be able to return there.

While on remand in Holloway, added Vincent, his wife had written
to him several times. 'Each letter from prison was devoted to Rob's
welfare,' he said. Dorothy had provided in her letters no explanation
for her crimes. 'My head is so bad – I don't think I can face it all again,'
she had written. Did she mean, face yet another court appearance? Her
husband took this to be her probable meaning. He had been surprised,
he said, to find her in court that day – and she, him. 'I shouldn't come
up if I were you,' she'd written. 'Who will look after Rob when you're
away? There'd be no one to save him if the house was bombed.'

Dorothy had apparently strayed from the subject of her pet retriever's
well-being only once more in her letters to her husband. 'Don't trouble
to dig up the garden. The 500 bulbs I planted last summer will come up
again,' she had told him. There wasn't much for Vincent O'Grady to
return home to as his wife said goodbye.

While, unsurprisingly, the news coverage of her appeal did not
match that given to her sensational conviction in December, it still
filled many column inches in the local and national British press – and
was of sufficient merit to attract the interest of news editors from as far
afield as the Antipodes. In Australia the *Melbourne Argus* headlined its
report, 'Husband's words to spy wife,' quoting Vincent's reassurance
to Dorothy: 'Don't worry. I'll be waiting for you. There'll always be a
home.' On the same day in New Zealand the *Evening Post* at Wellington
devoted space to report on the outcome of the 'woman traitor's'
Old Bailey hearing. Despite her husband's hopeful assertion to the

contrary, Dorothy O'Grady had *not* shaken off that stigma as she headed for jail.

The precise legal arguments used by John Scott Henderson to spare her life were, of course, unknown to all but a few in 1941, and would remain so for years to come. The public were aware only of the apparently inarguable fact that Dorothy O'Grady was to be locked up for a very long time, condemned still as a spy.

Her destination was the prison at Aylesbury, an early Victorian building, opened in 1845, which had initially served as Buckinghamshire's county jail before assuming the role of a women's prison in 1890. Apart from some isolated short transfers elsewhere for medical reasons, Dorothy would see out the war at Aylesbury and would remain there for the nine years she actually spent behind bars before being granted her release five years early in January 1950.

Those nine years in prison would prove both eventful and illuminating, but it would be several decades before the outside world was finally given full insight into this period of O'Grady's extraordinary life. Not only the evidence used to convict her, but also a plethora of revealing documents relating to her earlier life and subsequent imprisonment, were all, like Dorothy herself, locked away, their release forbidden by order of the Lord Chancellor as being 'contrary to the public interest, whether on security or other grounds'. Behind bars, out of sight, her infamy, if not forgotten, was progressively submerged beneath the tidal waves of terror, tragedy, toil and eventual triumph that captivated the British people until final victory was achieved by the Allied military forces in 1945, and the long process of rebuilding a war-weary nation held them in its grip.

On the Isle of Wight in the years immediately following the war, its residents surveyed the widespread structural damage in their midst and mourned the civilian and military victims of enemy action against their homeland. They spoke sometimes of Dorothy O'Grady, the housewife and seaside landlady who had lived among them for the first part of the conflict until she was caught and jailed – so far as they knew – as a Nazi agent. Whatever the extent of her treachery, while they, the people of

Wight, had made sacrifices, endured hardship and suffered loss during the six years of warfare, Dorothy O'Grady had done nothing to help the struggle for survival and, had fate not intervened, might well have contributed to the surrender of the island and its mother country.

On these issues the island's residents were left to conjecture, gossip and guesswork. But if ever Mrs O'Grady was to set foot on the Isle of Wight again she was guaranteed, at the very least, the most hostile of receptions. And so it was to prove.[5]

# Notes

1   The tenet that criminal legal aid should be granted whenever it was in the interests of justice to do so had been set by James Ramsay MacDonald's Labour government in 1930. A series of steps were taken subsequently – including setting up the first Citizens Advice Bureau in 1939 and the Rushcliffe Committee, which reported in 1945 on all aspects of providing legal help for people who could not afford it – before Clement Attlee's Labour administration introduced the first unified legal aid scheme in 1949.

2   John Scott Henderson (1895–1964) also had the distinction of serving for a period in the mid-1950s as head of the Inner Temple, one of the four Inns of Court (professional associations) for barristers and judges.

3   Sir Thomas Inskip, 1st Viscount Caldecote CBE, PC, KC (1876–1947), combined prominent legal and political careers. Called to the bar in 1899, he became a King's Counsel in 1914, was elected to Parliament as a Conservative in 1918, was knighted in 1922 and was raised to the peerage on the outbreak of war in 1939. Inskip served in several high-status legal and political posts, including those of Solicitor General (three times), Attorney General (twice), Minister for Co-ordination of Defence (controversially in 1936), Secretary of State for Dominion Affairs (twice), Lord Chancellor and Lord Chief Justice, the position he held between 1940 and 1946. As Viscount Caldecote, he also served for a brief period in 1940 as Leader of the House of Lords as well as leading the Conservatives in the Upper Chamber.

4   Sir Travers Humphreys KC (1867–1956), a noted barrister and judge, prominent in the English judiciary when he sat with Lord Caldecote at Dorothy O'Grady's appeal hearing, was the father of Christmas Humphreys QC, one of Britain's most high-profile legal figures in the latter half of the

twentieth century. Frederick Tucker (1888–1975), the third sitting judge at the O'Grady appeal, was a former Recorder of Southampton who was later created a life peer (as Baron Tucker) before his retirement in 1961.

5   Following the success of Dorothy O'Grady's appeal in February 1941, which saved her from the gallows, the unenviable distinction of being the first Briton to suffer execution under the Treachery Act fell to George Armstrong, hanged by Tom Pierrepoint at Wandsworth jail on 10 July 1941 (see Chapter 1).

# 6

# BETTER TO BE THOUGHT A FOOL THAN A TRAITOR

Vincent O'Grady had kept his word. Unwilling to stay on at Osborne Villa without the company of his wife, he had moved back to London (where he spent the majority of her time in prison), renting out the Sandown property in the post-war years. Vincent's health had begun to fail in the late 1940s. In 1949, aged 70, he had helped his wife petition for her early release from prison, principally so that she could look after him. When this was secured on Friday 24 February 1950, after she had served a little over nine years, he had returned to the Isle of Wight to welcome her back to the home he had, as promised, kept for her.

While the prison authorities had provided no obstacle to her early departure from Aylesbury, they were far from hopeful about her future prospects. They had delved deeply into the background, character and motivational forces that underpinned the life of Dorothy O'Grady. There was very good reason for them to express serious concern about the future for Britain's oddest convicted wartime spy – though this was something else that was set to remain hidden from wider awareness until the release to The National Archives in 2007 of the documents relating to her imprisonment and state of mind at the time she was freed.

With the probable exceptions of her husband and his unmarried sister, Agnes – who had lived with Vincent and Dorothy when the couple had first moved to the island in 1933, and had returned to Osborne Villa to help her brother when Dorothy was convicted in 1940 – nobody on the Isle of Wight had any real knowledge of the truth that lay behind the extraordinary O'Grady story. Thus, with the revealing records from prison locked away and destined to remain so for the following fifty-seven years, the ground was prepared in 1950 for the shifting sands of opinion that would increasingly define the story up to and beyond Dorothy's death.

It took her just a matter of days to start the tongues wagging again after she walked free from prison on that Friday morning in February. Before heading back to Sandown, Dorothy made for an address in London with a mission long planned while she was incarcerated at Aylesbury. Her destination was Fleet Street and her mission was to give her favourite newspaper, the *Sunday Express*, an exclusive that was surely quite unlike anything it had published before.

'Immediately on release she came to the *Sunday Express* where she told an almost incredible story,' wrote journalist Sidney Rodin in his account of the interview he conducted with O'Grady. His use of the adverb 'almost' was probably unnecessary. Added Rodin, 'She said that, in fact, she had never done any spying, that the whole episode was "a huge joke" – a piece of exhibitionism on her part. That being sentenced to death gave her the biggest thrill in her life.'

A joke? A thrill? It beggared belief. But Rodin's smiling interviewee was keen to point out that this was nothing particularly out of the ordinary for her. The *Sunday Express* reporter sensibly refrained from comment, resorting instead to the simplest of strategies. 'Let Mrs O'Grady tell her story in her own words,' he wrote.

Dorothy, it would emerge many years later, had compiled a written draft while in jail of her entire life story – or at least the edited version she wanted people to know about. The *Sunday Express* was always the intended recipient. Rodin was the first of many journalists over the course of the next four decades who would listen in astonishment bordering on disbelief as the chirpy little woman recounted her tale. Like all those who followed him, he had no way of knowing that key elements of the story were being omitted. Still, he had plenty to write about.

'Since I was a child I have loved to make up tales and pretend I have done things that I have not done, out of love of shocking people,' was Dorothy's opening quote. What followed no doubt shocked most of the *Sunday Express*'s readers.

'At school I once wrote on pieces of paper that I had killed my mother,' she continued in chillingly disturbing manner. 'I hid them about the place, hoping they would be found and that they would hang me. Yet, I was very fond of my mother.'

Having sketched in the background to the extreme nature of this self-confessed character flaw, Dorothy described how it had influenced her behaviour in wartime.

'When the war began all my guests left Osborne Villa and my husband, who is now 72, took a fireman's job in London. I was all alone except for my black retriever, Rob,' she said – oddly adding a year to husband Vincent's real age of 71.

Describing the newly bolstered military presence on the Isle of Wight in 1940 – 'full of soldiers ... emplacements everywhere' – and the evasion tactics she adopted to outwit the army, reach the forbidden beaches and provide Rob with the means to bathe in the sea, she then recounted the key events that led to her capture.

In essence, the outline she provided for the *Sunday Express* of the fateful encounter on Yaverland beach which culminated in her military arrest was the story she would gleefully re-tell in her many later press interviews. Though in detail her accounts were seldom entirely consistent, Sidney Rodin was the first journalist to hear, and duly report, a particularly bizarre strand of the tale which O'Grady would many times repeat and which is now an integral part of her legend.

'They asked me what I was doing there,' she said, recalling the approach of the two soldiers who found her sitting on the zoned-off beach in the August sunshine. 'And then one of them, a sergeant, noticed a small paper swastika pinned under the lapel of my coat. It came from the *Daily Express* war map, with which little coloured flags were provided for marking the changes in the [war] front.'

Dorothy's explanation was plausible – but only just. 'The swastika flag must have stuck to my hair as I bent down to pick something up in front of the map. As I walked I felt it in my hair and quite naturally pulled it out and put it under my lapel.'

So there she was – sitting brazenly in a militarily sensitive area, barred to the public, with the barely concealed emblem of the enemy pinned to her clothing. It was hardly the behaviour of a genuine Nazi spy, but was arguably in keeping with the actions of a mischievous fantasist intent on arousing suspicion that she was working for the other side. Yet, according to Dorothy O'Grady in 1950, the idea of playing the part of a spy for a laugh had not occurred to her at that juncture.

There was no mention of her attempt at bribing the soldiers – even though this was a fact, one she would happily talk about in later accounts – and she made only fleeting reference to her interview at Bembridge with their commanding officer, saying, 'He checked up on me with the police at Sandown and then let me go.'

It was not until the local police called on her, added Dorothy, that she took a snap decision to adopt, as best she could, the persona of an enemy agent:

> A young policeman came to question me some time afterwards. He asked my views on Hitler. I realised that they thought me a spy. I said to myself: 'Very well, I'll give them something to think about.' So I told the constable that I thought Hitler was a fine man and, if he wanted to make Germany greater, I didn't see why he shouldn't. To my huge delight, the constable wrote all of this down.

The die was cast. 'Now I began to enter into the lark in earnest,' the unashamedly jovial Dorothy told Sidney Rodin. 'I had guide maps of the island, which I used to give to my guests, and I began marking them with military objectives.'

Collating the island's military information was always going to be a hazardous business. Not because of the obvious risk of being caught. That, it seemed, wouldn't have mattered at all. However, snooping on military sites on the Isle of Wight in the summer of 1940 was asking for trouble from both sides in the conflict.

'I was nearly a casualty in a daylight bombing attack on the Royal Marine Hotel, Ventnor. I bought a postcard showing the hotel which I marked for I knew it stood above a military billet,' she said, revealing her presence in the town on 19 August when the Royal Marine, once one of the island's most prestigious hotels, was seriously damaged by the enemy. A noteworthy 'hit' for the Luftwaffe, perhaps, but its real target in the Ventnor area was the RAF's radar station on St Boniface Down, and that had already been attacked – twice – by German planes in August 1940, in the week before Dorothy was snooping in the town.[1]

Had she been aware of the vital strategic role the radar station was playing in Britain's desperate struggle for survival at the height of the Battle of Britain? She certainly gave that impression to Rodin. 'I went to St Boniface Down ... where there was a secret radar station, and made rough pencil sketches of the layout, one of which I dropped near the sentry,' she informed her interviewer. It can probably be regarded as unlikely that this visit took place on 12 August, when the station was first attacked, or four days later when the Luftwaffe swooped again on the already seriously crippled radar facility. If she had been there on either of those days, she would have been lucky to escape with her life.

Further up the Isle of Wight's south-eastern coast, she discovered that a flight of stone steps leading down to the beach at Luccombe Chine had been partly blasted away to prevent public access. To Dorothy O'Grady this was a challenge rather than a deterrent. 'Exploring with my dog ... I found a narrow, twisting path which enabled me to descend to the beach and climb up again,' she said.

Clearly, the detail was ingrained firmly in her mind. 'I made three sketches of this place, including the path with access and showing a trench which was manned by soldiers at night, even indicating the number and the time they went on duty – and a camouflaged gun which I had seen on a housetop above the beach.

'Other sketches I made included those of the naval wireless station at Culver Cliff and the sea fort where a big naval gun had just been installed,' added Dorothy.[2]

It would, she hoped, provide telling information with profound consequences for the intended recipients of her snooping endeavours – not the enemy waiting to pounce across the Channel, but those tasked with the job of keeping them out. 'Most of these sketches I dropped where soldiers would find them, but I always carried some more, and a marked map of the island, in my handbag to keep up the illusion of being a spy should I be arrested ... I longed to be arrested.'

She had, of course, already been arrested once, by the military, and questioned by the police. So how had she reacted to the arrival on her doormat of the police summonses ordering her appearance before the magistrates in Ryde for breaching the Defence Regulations – the two charges arising from her brush with the army at Yaverland? Dorothy did not reprise her 'too scared to attend' line for Sidney Rodin. The clear implication from the *Sunday Express* interview was that she deliberately ignored the summonses so that she could prolong her spying 'lark'.

Succinctly, she told Rodin of her flight from justice: 'I packed a bag, locked up the villa and went to stay at Alum Bay. I was three weeks there before they found me. All the time I kept marking my maps and dropping my little swastikas.'

Her apparent confusion between Alum Bay and nearby Totland Bay – her real bolt-hole while on the run – can no doubt be put down to a minor memory lapse. More intriguing was her omission of any reference to cutting military telephone wires during her sojourn in the West Wight, the subject of one of the capital charges under the Treachery Act which very nearly cost Dorothy her life. Why, in full confessional flow, had she left this out? Did she feel that, unlike her map-making and sketching, the act of severing vital communication links had been altogether more serious – something she couldn't simply laugh off?[3]

In fact, Dorothy had told Rodin relatively little about her stay in the island's far west – much of which remains something of a mystery to this day – and had said nothing about the circumstances of her arrest by the police at the Totland guest house. But her tale was far from finished. She picked it up at the point where the arresting police officers had taken her to the police station in Yarmouth.

'They found my maps and sketches in my handbag, and also a false identity card,' she recounted with impish glee. 'I thought I had lost my card a few months before and obtained a new one. Then I found the old one and took great delight in rubbing out my name and substituting a false one with a London address.'

Skipping through the subsequent court hearings on the Isle of Wight, she spoke at length of the three months she spent on remand at Holloway jail prior to her trial. There, she said, she had been 'interrogated for long periods,' and added, 'My chief interrogator from MI5 kept asking to whom I gave my information. I refused to say. Earlier, however, I had made up the yarn that a submarine used to appear off the Isle of Wight at night and a man came ashore in a rubber dinghy.' This, she had told her interrogators, had been her contact with the enemy.

Whether MI5 actually believed any of this or not, she had talked herself into deep trouble. 'When I knew I was going to be tried at Winchester I became a little frightened and was almost on the point of confessing that the whole thing was a joke. But I hardened and looked forward to the trial as an immense thrill.'

She'd admitted to Rodin that, during the two-day trial, 'right inside me I was scared,' but then made it clear that any deep-seated fear of what might happen to her had not spoilt her fun. 'I enjoyed every minute of it,' she said. 'I learned that, because of my maps, most of the defence plans for the island had been changed.'

It is not hard to imagine Sidney Rodin's incredulity as Dorothy reached the climax of her fantastical tale. 'The excitement of being tried for my life was intense,' she told him:

The supreme moment came when an official stood behind the judge and put on his black cap for him before he pronounce the death sentence. The man didn't put it on straight. It went over one of the judge's eyes and looked so funny that I was giggling inside and had a job not to laugh. It was hard to keep a straight face and look serious and solemn as I knew a spy should.

But the thrill of being condemned to die as an enemy agent was, Dorothy added, somewhat offset by the precise wording of Mr Justice Macnaghten's pronouncement. 'I found it disappointing that I was going to be hanged instead of shot.'

More bad news was soon to follow for Dorothy. Earnestly she told Rodin, 'My next disappointment was to learn that they would put a hood over my head and tie my hands behind my back before taking me to the scaffold, This upset me. I protested, "What is the good of being hanged if I can't see what is happening?" ...'

Her next remark, however, betrayed a hint that the bravado was perhaps bolstered by an underlying belief that, despite the trial judge's dire sentence, she would avoid execution: 'Sometimes I said, "They won't hang a woman in Britain." I took some persuading to appeal against the death sentence and I spent Christmas in the death cell. They gave me a little piece of Christmas pudding, a few sweets and some cake.' For the first time in Dorothy O'Grady's extraordinary account of her 1940 story, a degree of poignancy had crept into the tale.[4]

It was immediately replaced by another helping of O'Grady mischief. 'I used to spin the officers all sorts of yarns about my spying. All these, I discovered, were later written down.' Was this further evidence of a woman secure in the knowledge, or at least belief, that, whatever she said, she would not be hanged? It was – and remains – hard to gauge. Her next revelation to Rodin suggested that, in truth, she believed execution in January 1941 was still very much on the cards.

'My only fear was that I would be taken away one morning to be hanged without having been told the night before' – presumably because this would have deprived her of the ultimate anticipatory thrill. 'Sometimes I dreaded going to sleep in case this happened. I was terrified, yet I enjoyed being terrified.'

Could all of this really have been true? If it was, it pointed clearly to one inarguable truism – Dorothy O'Grady had exposed herself as a woman very far from normal.

Granted, apparently against her own wishes, the right to appeal – and at least a stay of execution – she had another day in court to anticipate when, in February 1941, the hearing was heard at the Old Bailey. It was evidently a huge disappointment. 'Three judges heard my appeal ... it hurt me that not once did any of them turn to look at me. When I was sentenced to 14 years' imprisonment I became almost hysterical and could not stop crying all that night.'

So she had begun her jail sentence at Aylesbury the next day in a state of abject misery. Did this persuade her to come clean and admit that, in reality, she was nothing more sinister than a thrill-seeking prankster? Apparently not. 'For many months I told no-one that my spying was a mere pretence.' According to Dorothy, the mask did not finally slip until, prompted either by conscience or self-interest – she did not tell Rodin which of the two it was – she wrote to her husband 'explaining everything for the first time'. Although this had been penned in the form of a personal message to Vincent O'Grady, inevitably it amounted to an open confession. The letter was intercepted by staff at the prison.

While the 'truth' was now revealed, it was not until she had spent a full two years in prison that Dorothy O'Grady made it official. 'I wrote out a full confession. It was sent to the Home Secretary,' her account continued. 'My statement concluded with the words, "I know I acted foolishly but I did not realise the gravity of my acts at the time." The Home Secretary acknowledged my communication and said it would be filed with the documents relating to my case.'

That was as far as it got. The years rolled by. She waited in vain for some formal recognition of her belated honesty. 'The war ended and I still heard nothing.'

Her status – and, indeed, her mood – had, however, evidently changed for the better. 'After three years I had become a "special" prisoner with many privileges. The "specials" have their own small wing, with sitting room, kitchen and a very nice garden. I became quite happy in prison. My husband visited me regularly.'

But, as her time at Aylesbury grew ever longer, her concern for Vincent's well-being increased to disrupt her prison idyll. 'He had stood by me through all the years and kept our home together, but he was getting old and I felt I should make one more effort to be released so that I could come out and look after him.'

So, in November 1949, she had petitioned the Home Secretary for her release. 'I wrote, "My husband is now 72 and wants me at home. I know I did wrong in pretending to be a spy, but I have paid for it now." The answer came on 15 February.'

Home Secretary James Chuter Ede had ordered her almost immediate release. Nine days later she had left Aylesbury and set course for home – via Fleet Street, 'That,' Sidney Rodin confirmed, 'is the story as Mrs O'Grady told it to me.'

But the *Sunday Express* man couldn't possibly have left it there. A burning question remained unanswered. Dorothy O'Grady was abnormal – that much was palpably obvious – but did it go further than that? Was she clinically insane?

Rodin was, of course, no expert in mental illness, but he had clearly done his best to resolve the issue. 'Readers who may doubt her sanity should know that at no material time has it been doubted,' he wrote:

> When she had been in prison four years she was seen by Dr Jean Durrant, a psychiatrist. Dr Durrant is not at liberty to discuss individual cases. But when I saw her at home in Chelsea she said to me, 'No person certified as insane would be kept at Holloway or Aylesbury.' So what further light can Mrs O'Grady herself throw on her affair?[5]

Unsurprisingly, the talkative Mrs O'Grady *did* have quite a lot to say on her own state of mind. With what Rodin judged to be 'complete frankness', she had told him, 'Perhaps I have some sort of kink which took hold of me at the time because I was alone amid the continual noise of guns and the droning of planes.'

Loneliness, insularity and low self-esteem, she emphasised, had characterised her development since childhood:

> All my life I had never been anything. I had always been insignificant. I never had a close friend, even at school. I felt tremendously bucked when I saw that they thought me clever enough to be a spy. It made me feel somebody instead of being an ordinary seaside landlady. Yet I was astonished when they believed it all. I never imagined they would.

And now, she added, she was keen to reverse that process. It was time to set the record straight. 'I consider it better that people on the Isle of Wight who doubted me should now know the truth. Better to be thought a fool than a traitor.'

But was it really the truth? Or had Dorothy O'Grady spun Sidney Rodin yet another of her mischievous tales as insurance against the probability of a hostile reception back home on the Isle of Wight? No doubt with this in mind, Rodin had sought official clarification from those at the government department who would certainly have the answer – should they choose to divulge it. Hopefully, he'd sent a copy of his O'Grady interview to the Home Office.

An official told him, 'The question whether Mrs O'Grady's explanation of her conduct is feasible is not one on which the Home Office can properly express an opinion as she was tried in open court.' This was, of course, factually incorrect – Dorothy's trial and appeal had both been held in secret – but the message was clear. The Home Office was not going to shed any light on the matter.

Rodin had one more point of note to record as he concluded his lengthy O'Grady exclusive: 'In the history of Aylesbury jail, no woman has ever served so long a sentence. not even those in "for life". They are usually released after five years.'

For the moment – and for a great many years to come – Dorothy O'Grady had absolute control of her story. The questions relating to her mental state and the veracity of her incredible account would remain unanswered until the closing years of the twentieth century and, in several key respects, right up to the present day.

So Dorothy walked away from the *Sunday Express* anticipating her soon to be established reputation as a fantasising, story-telling thrill-seeker who somehow had fooled the combined intellect of Britain's police, military, legal and intelligence services into thinking she was a Nazi spy. She was prepared for people to think her foolish – probably realising that the less charitable might regard her as mad – but, as she had said, it was the lesser evil than to return home with the status of a woman who had betrayed her country at a time of peril.

Yet the facts remained. She had certainly collected militarily sensitive information which might have proved very useful to the enemy had they got their hands on it (and in 1950 the public were totally in the dark as to whether they had or not) and, while she had not actually admitted as much, she had been convicted of threatening the defence of the island by cutting the military telephone wires. It was unlikely that forgiveness on the Isle of Wight would be easily won. She could only hope that Sidney Rodin's report of their meeting would be prominently placed in the *Sunday Express* and would soften public animosity. On Saturday 4 March 1950 she took the ferry back to the Isle of Wight.

When the article appeared the following day Dorothy may well have been pleased that her story had made the front page – or possibly disappointed that it was not the lead story, shunted into second place by the tragically dramatic news of a terrified Yugoslav man's fatal leap from an aircraft on a deportation flight from Britain. Still, Rodin's O'Grady piece was splashed across three columns, spilling out across another three as it continued on an inside news page, and Dorothy's suitably smiling face, in a newly taken photograph, dominated the front page beneath a bold three-deck headline – 'Women says she had herself sentenced to death for "a huge joke"' – and the page's only reporter byline.

Would it bring smiles to the faces of the island community she was about to rejoin?

Vincent O'Grady's sister, Agnes, had returned once more to Osborne Villa to help Dorothy's readjustment to life away from the institutionalised environment she had grown accustomed to at Aylesbury. It was, however, soon obvious that, despite her newspaper interview, it was not going to be easy for Dorothy back home in Sandown. The sense of betrayal lingered among the local population. Some were astonished that 'the spy' had returned to live among them. Many were angered by her renewed presence in the town. They wanted nothing to do with her.

There are stories that, whether or not the townsfolk believed her to be a traitor, she encountered a great deal of difficulty with even the most basic of social interaction. One Sandown resident, a young girl at the time, recalled being in her father's tobacconist's shop when Dorothy, very soon after her return, walked in to buy cigarettes. The shopkeeper was pretty sure that he recognised his visitor.

'You'd be Mrs O'Grady?' he asked.

'Indeed I am, sir,' replied Dorothy in her high-pitched voice.

'There's the door, madam,' said the shopkeeper, refusing to serve her, pointing to the exit.

'As soon as she had left, my dad was on the phone to all the other tobacconists in the area. "The woman's out!" he told them,' recalled the former Sandown schoolgirl.

## Notes

1  The site of the Royal Marine Hotel at Ventnor is now partly occupied by Royal Marine House, a modern development of holiday apartments.

2  Dorothy O'Grady did not specify which of the four eastern Solent sea forts she had sketched in 1940. The probability is that it was St Helens Fort, the nearest to the island's north-eastern coast, located only a short distance from Culver. However, it was the army's responsibility to man the forts, not the Royal Navy's.

3  O'Grady never admitted cutting the telephone wires in any of her many later interviews (see Chapter 7).

4   O'Grady's apparent belief that a woman would not be hanged in Britain
    was at odds with the facts. Fourteen women had suffered the death penalty in
    the UK between the turn of the twentieth century and the outbreak of the
    Second World War, the most recent being Charlotte Bryant (33), hanged in
    July 1936 for the murder (by poisoning) of her husband. Four other women
    would be executed after the war, with Ruth Ellis (28) the very last woman to
    be hanged – in July 1955 – for the fatal shooting of her lover, David Blakely.
5   Dr Durrant was actually employed as a psychotherapist at HMP Holloway
    (see Chapter 12).

# 7

# THE GIGGLE THAT WAS TAKEN TO THE GRAVE

Time would prove to be a very slow healer, but Dorothy O'Grady somehow managed to weather the storm of her hotly controversial return to Sandown. In the summer of 1951 she, Vincent and Agnes O'Grady were welcoming guests once more to Osborne Villa's boarding accommodation. However, echoing the false hopes in the O'Grady household of the final pre-war summer twelve years earlier, this was the start of a period of domestic calm that lasted for just two years.

It was particularly cruel on Vincent O'Grady that, after he had waited so long for his wife's return, his health should very quickly deteriorate until, in August 1953, he was admitted to St Mary's Hospital in Newport, the Isle of Wight's capital, having suffered a stroke. He died there on the 27th of that month, the causes of his death formally noted as cerebral arteriosclerosis (hardening of the arteries) and senility. Among the obituaries in Sandown's local newspaper, the *Isle of Wight Chronicle*, the following week there was not a mention of the former Royal Navy rating and senior firefighter who had served his country with some distinction – merely a three-line notice of his passing in the classified columns, for which Dorothy had presumably paid. Strangely, in line with the formal registration of his death, and the subsequent death certificate, this recorded Vincent's age as 76. It was an error. He was actually two years younger.

There is sufficient documentation to prove that Vincent Henry O'Grady was born on 21 December 1878 at 16 Red Lion Square, Holborn, in central London, the second eldest child of Joseph, a constable serving with the Metropolitan Police, and Hannah O'Grady (née Coffey), who had married in the city's West Ham district four years before Vincent's arrival. While Hannah was a Londoner, born in East Ham, Joseph hailed from the Gloucestershire town of Cheltenham. By the time the national census for 1891 was taken (when Vincent was 12), the family had moved to Sutton, Surrey, in London's south-western suburbs, and there were six children, their ages ranging from 2 to 14. Agnes O'Grady (6 years old) was the second youngest when the census was taken.[1]

Ten years later, when the next census was compiled, Vincent had left the family home and was boarding at lodgings in Gillingham, Kent, a town conveniently close to the Royal Navy dockyard at Chatham, where the 22-year-old was serving as a naval rating – just as his father had done, albeit briefly, three decades earlier. Vincent had joined the navy in August 1896 as a boy seaman, initially aboard the moored hulk of a former destroyer converted for use as a boys' training ship. In January 1897, having reached the age of 18 after a satisfactory period of training, he was eligible to enlist as an adult, becoming an ordinary seaman and signing up for twelve years' naval service. At this point his service record noted that he was a little over 5ft 4in tall – he had grown just half-an-inch since arriving at Chatham – with black hair, blue eyes and a dark complexion. Vincent progressed to the status of able seaman in 1898 and then to what would prove his ultimate naval rank, that of leading seaman, in 1903.[2]

If he had joined the Royal Navy to see the world, Vincent was probably disappointed to spend a significant proportion of his naval service aboard HMS *Pembroke*, once a 101-gun first rater (when she was known as HMS *Duncan*) which had been relegated to harbour service in 1890; the screw-driven yacht tender HMS *Wildfire*, a base ship since

1889; and the corvette HMS *Dido*, which had been reduced to a hulk a decade before the start of Vincent's naval career.

For brief periods he was a crew member aboard the battleships HMS *Victorious* and *Revenge*, both launched in the 1890s, and the cruiser HMS *Galatea*. It hardly amounted to a glamorous career at sea, but Vincent acquitted himself well. Consistently, his character and conduct as a sailor were rated 'very good'. However, he cut short his Royal Navy service by five years, buying himself out in February 1904, but remained at sea, based at Chatham, for a short while after a seamless transfer to the recently formed civilian-manned Royal Fleet Auxiliary.

Then, in 1906, began Vincent O'Grady's unbroken twenty-six-year career with the London Fire Brigade, which saw him serve at various fire stations before, during and for more than a decade following the First World War. It was as a firefighter, stationed in the city's East End at Bethnal Green, that Vincent, aged 47, married the 29-year-old Dorothy on 21 August 1926. The ceremony took place at the register office in Maldon, the old town at the head of the Blackwater estuary in Essex, where Dorothy had been living under her maiden name of Squire at 39 Cherry Gardens Road. Vincent's profession as a London firefighter was duly noted on the marriage certificate. All that appeared in the 'rank or profession' box alongside Dorothy's name was an enigmatic diagonal line.

Her most recent line of work prior to the wedding would no doubt have been regarded by all concerned as particularly unsuitable for inclusion on a marriage certificate. But this, and the remainder of the trouble-strewn path which had led Dorothy to Maldon Register Office, was yet another part of the O'Grady jigsaw to remain hidden away for seven decades, known only to those who had a part to play in her arrest, conviction and consequent imprisonment in the 1940s.

She left Maldon to live with her husband in east London until Vincent retired, aged 54, from the fire brigade, subsequently supplementing his half-pay pension by working as a fire inspector in the private sector – a job which meant he was away from home for long periods. To remedy this, and to fulfill an apparently long-held dream of moving to the Isle of Wight, the couple decamped from London to take up an initial tenancy at Osborne Villa in 1933, moving again on its termination in 1936 to 44 New Road, Lake, where they remained for the next two years. Returning briefly to London, they were back on the island as owners and guest house proprietors of Osborne Villa in June 1939.[3,4]

Events since 1939, of course, had been just about as far removed as possible from the hoped-for fantasy of running a seaside boarding house in retirement. The war, and Dorothy's decidedly dubious role in it, had wreaked havoc. But now, with Vincent's passing, and the departure from Sandown soon afterwards of Agnes O'Grady, Dorothy entered a period of relative anonymity, her wartime notoriety no longer of major concern locally as the years drifted by. Remaining at Osborne Villa, though no longer running it as a guest house, Dorothy lived alone for a short time. Then, in 1954, she began taking in long-term boarders at the house rather than the short-stay holidaymakers who previously had been accommodated there. A glance at the electoral registers from the 1950s and early 1960s reveals the names, at various stages, of up to four other adults listed alongside her own as Osborne Villa's residents. Some clearly stayed for years.[5]

Dorothy no doubt entertained them regularly with tales of her wartime 'spying lark' – but the audience was inevitably small. Too small. When the chances came to remind the nation as a whole of how she, the plain ordinary Mrs O'Grady, had fooled MI5 et al. as part of a hugely enjoyable high-risk prank, she needed little persuasion. Periodically, the journalists – and others with an interest in her amazing story, such as the noted author and espionage specialist Bernard Newman – would call on her to check for themselves whether it could really have been the truth. She was pleased to tell them all that it certainly had been.

Soon after reviving the interest once more via an article in the popular weekly tabloid *Reveille*, Dorothy was recounting her tale yet again for the country's favourite new medium, television. In 1962 she was interviewed for the BBC's regional news programme, *South at Six* (forerunner of the present *South Today*) by Peter Hill. A former naval intelligence officer, Hill was particularly well equipped to handle the assignment. His assessment of Dorothy's tale would therefore carry some weight. In his filmed encounter with her, she admitted – as, in essence, she'd been doing since 1950 – that it had been a case of her becoming 'carried away with the excitement of being thought a spy during the war, but the trouble was, they believed me. I never thought they would believe me'.

Somewhat true to form, Dorothy revealed to Peter Hill that she had been upset by the *Reveille* article. Had she been misrepresented in the piece? Had they not believed her story? No, it wasn't that. *Reveille* had described Rob, the retriever dog at the heart of her 1940 epic, as a spaniel. This, in Dorothy's eyes, was a disgrace!

But, in preparing his film, Hill did coax detail from her that was altogether new. Dorothy told him she had intended to tell the truth in the witness box, but was never given the chance to do so. 'I wanted to tell counsel,' she said in a taped interview. 'I knew that, if I just told the truth, it would be all right ...' But, according to her, John Scott Henderson, her counsel, had no time to talk with her – 'he said he had another case due' – and was interested only in one thing. 'He said, "get her to sign a paper saying she will not give evidence or I will not take the case up – I will not be a party to perjury." Then he had to rush off. So, when I went in court, I never said a word ... I never even spoke to counsel.'

According to Dorothy, then, a somewhat disinterested and distracted John Scott Henderson had clearly not trusted her to tell the truth on oath, whatever story she came up with. But was she now telling the truth to Peter Hill in recounting this?

Looking back on the interview more than thirty years later in an article he wrote for the *British Journalism Review*, Hill remembered that at times it had been hard to work out when she was telling the truth. He added that, when she had told him that she had 'giggled' when the trial judge's black cap had slipped sideways as he was about to pronounce the death sentence, 'I recall doubting her complete sanity. She said she was interested to know what it felt like to be hanged.'

But Peter Hill made clear that he believed the substance of her story. He was convinced of it. She had certainly trespassed on the forbidden beaches, she had clearly made maps and sketches of military installations and she had almost certainly cut the telephone lines. She had broken Defence Regulations, wasted much police time and impaired the defence of the island. But, as she had insisted to him, Rodin and everyone else who interviewed her, it was all a pretence. She had done it not for the benefit of the Third Reich, but to please herself.

Despite the media attention, there were now some people on the Isle of Wight, more than ten years after O'Grady returned there from prison, who knew nothing of her past. Nursing auxiliary Ruth Powell was among them when, in the early 1960s, the ageing Dorothy's name appeared on a list of patients she had been detailed to visit by the sister-in-charge at a Sandown medical practice. 'I had not been told anything about her other than she was a very nice lady,' recalled the now retired nurse – Ruth Gazzard today – many years later:

> I had come from Twickenham and had been seconded to Sandown, so I had very little local knowledge. I used to help her wash and dress in the mornings, so I went inside Osborne Villa, into her sitting room, several times. She seemed quite pleasant to me. I didn't notice anything odd about her – nor about the house.

Yet, it is clear from the recollection of another local nurse that, as late as 1973, Dorothy had still not succeeded in casting off the cloak of a wartime traitor. 'I was on night duty at Shanklin Cottage Hospital where Mrs O'Grady had come into the medical ward as a patient,' Pauline Guildford remembered in 2011. 'I recall that she was sitting right up in the corner of the lounge all by herself. I asked the ward sister, why was nobody talking to her? "She's the spy," Sister told me.'[6]

By then, her health beginning to falter, Dorothy had finally moved from Osborne Villa, though not from Sandown. In 1963 she had gone to live close by at 6 Royal Crescent, a large house she shared with up to six other adults. Then, early in the 1970s, she had moved again to the newly opened Porter Court sheltered housing complex in Flitcroft Gardens, Lake, still less than a mile from her former guest house. Her new flatlet, No. 16, was one of fifty-four at the warden-supported block then owned and managed by South Wight Borough Council.

Among those who visited her there was Rob Atkins, who regularly delivered her groceries:

> I remember that some of her fellow residents clearly had it in for her. They told me, 'don't be nice to her, she's a wicked woman'. Personally, I got on well with her, she was always pleasant to me. At first she didn't say anything about what had happened to her in the war, but later she did open up. She said she had done it just to trick and irritate people because she was being stopped from going on the beach. But she hadn't been a real spy. It was all made up.

Mr Atkins, who now works at Porter Court as a mental health nurse, added that Dorothy had told him her oft-repeated story about finding it hard not to laugh as she was sentenced to death when the judge's black cap slipped over his face. Interestingly, he recalled that 'she was a bit racist about black people, like quite a few of her generation at that time, I suppose, but I also remember that she was very religious. The vicar used to call regularly there to give her communion.'

While the blaze of her wartime infamy was never fully extinguished, it was reduced to little more than a flicker in the 1970s, the passage of time, and a prolonged lack of refreshed national exposure, inevitably increasing the levels of ignorance and indifference on the part of the public. That it was so spectacularly re-ignited in her declining years was largely down to Dorothy herself – her reported wartime reserve once more fully submerged beneath an apparent desire for social contact and recognition. Settled in her flatlet home at Lake, she had plenty of time to talk of times past, an irresistible urge to do so – to be the centre of attention – and a captive audience among her fellow residents.

After all, she had long ceased to be a woman of insignificance. She was Dorothy O'Grady, the mistress of wartime deception. Perhaps she thought it was time to remind people of that; time to 'go public' again with her terrific tale; time to make clear once more, in her eighty-fourth year, that she had never been a traitor. Maybe she thought she might not get another chance. And so the press, both nationally and locally, came again to her aid. It was still a sublime feature story.

In 1981 Dorothy welcomed reporters and photographers to her flatlet and both entertained and flabbergasted them all with what would turn out to be her final interviews.

As she spoke in turn to the *Sunday Times* and local journalists, her core message was subtly different to that expressed in her earlier interviews. She had apparently given up any hope of being entirely redeemed in the eyes of the public. 'I have learned to accept that people are never going to forgive me for being convicted of spying,' said Dorothy, but she remained adamant on the crucial point. 'I never was a traitor. I had a fair trial but I got myself into trouble through being an exhibitionist. I wanted to be noticed. I wanted to shock people and be talked about.' Once more she stressed, 'I was never a spy.'

She was keen, yet again, to paint the picture of a woman whose life had been full of dull routine before she posed as a spy 'for a giggle and the excitement'. There was no reason for any journalist in 1981 to doubt this depiction of her pre-war life; it continued to give an element of plausibility to the rest of her story.

This, by now very well rehearsed, chapter she told in much the same chatty, smiling manner she had always adopted in her press interviews. Of course, it all sounded weirdly far-fetched but, as the *Isle of Wight Weekly Post* told its readers, 'the cheerful 84-year-old, who looks like everyone's idea of a silver-haired, favourite granny, clothed it with a certain credibility'. She had loved all the importance she felt when people thought her a spy. 'They looked up to me,' she said.

Bored and lonely, seeking adventure, excitement and a status she had never previously enjoyed. This again was the essence of Dorothy O'Grady's testament in 1981, her explanation for the events which nearly led to her execution and left her languishing in prison for the best part of a decade. 'Most people would emerge from that harrowing experience embittered, broken and permanently scarred,' noted the *Weekly Post*'s double-page feature spread on 10 April. 'But chuckling

Dorothy O'Grady, the spy who never was, says almost unbelievably, "It was the greatest adventure of my life. Some people *write* books. I *lived* mine" ...'

She acknowledged willingly and cheerfully to the journalists who called on her in the 1981 spring that she had done 'all the things we were forbidden. I went on barred sections of beaches, wore paper swastika badges, made sketches of military objectives – and dropped them near sentries'. In these, and other, key respects, her story was pretty much as before, as was her delight in recounting it.

A few additional nuggets were thrown to her interviewers. Taking her dog for walks on the cliffs at night, her handbag stuffed with her maps and sketches, Dorothy said she had deliberately used a torch in defiance of the wartime blackout regulations, hoping, with some justification, that this would enhance her chances of being arrested as a spy. If this were true, it said very little for the efficiency of the local ARP wardens. Whatever they thought of her, flashing a torch during the blackout, especially in a militarily sensitive area, was a serious matter.

As, of course, was not turning up for her scheduled court appearance at Ryde in that far-off summer. This time round, Dorothy had a new explanation: 'The first bus arrived an hour too early, the next an hour too late.' So she had hopped on another bus and travelled instead all the way to Totland Bay at the other end of the island. 'On a whim,' she explained. She had just fancied the ride.

Dorothy spoke about the proprietor of Latton House who provided her with temporary lodgings in Totland, noting, without a trace of rancour, that the landlady had later given evidence against her in court. As, naturally, had the police officers who arrested her in the guest house toilet. In at least one of the 1981 interviews she re-set the bizarre discovery of the swastika flag behind her lapel at Totland, rather than at her earlier military arrest on Yaverland beach. 'I was with one of the policemen when the wind blew my lapel forward and he saw it,' Dorothy explained, 'but it was not what he thought it was.' Then her story returned to the consistency of her earlier interpretations – the *Daily Express* war map, its national flags which were moved in line with

*Right*: Prisoner 7250: Dorothy O'Grady, aged 20 – her initial prison photographs, taken at HMP Holloway in 1918. Her use of the alias Pamela Arland, noted on the pictures, was repeated in 1940. (The National Archives)

*Left*: Dorothy O'Grady as photographed for the *Sunday Express* soon after she left prison in 1950 – on the day she gave reporter Sidney Rodin the first of her many extraordinary post-war interviews, claiming her wartime spying had been 'a joke'. (*Sunday Express*)

*Below*: The marriage certificate recording the register office union between London firefighter Vincent O'Grady, aged 47, and the 29-year-old Dorothy Squire at Maldon, Essex, in August 1926. The 'rank or profession' of Dorothy, who had just been released from prison for soliciting in London, was expediently omitted. (Author's collection)

CERTIFIED COPY OF AN ENTRY OF MARRIAGE    GIVEN AT THE GENERAL REGISTER OFFICE

Application Number 2289952-1

| No. | When Married | Name and Surname | Age | Condition | Rank or Profession | Residence at the time of Marriage | Father's Name and Surname | Rank or Profession of Father |
|---|---|---|---|---|---|---|---|---|
| 15 | Twenty-first august 1926 | Vincent Henry O'Grady | 47 years | Bachelor | Fireman (L.C.C. Fire Brigade) | Fire Station Green Street Bethnal Green | Joseph Benedict O'Grady (deceased) | Insurance agent |
|  |  | Dorothy Pamela Squire | 29 years | Spinster |  | 39 Cherry Gardens Maldon | George Squire (deceased) | Civil servant |

Married in the Register Office according to the Rites and Ceremonies of the _____ by Licence before me,

This Marriage was solemnized between us, { V. H. O'Grady / D. P. Squire } in the Presence of us, { C. M. Mead. / John R. Trollope } R. Sturm, Deputy Registrar. Alfred W. Freeman, Supt. Registrar.

CERTIFIED to be a true copy of an entry in the certified copy of a register of Marriages in the Registration District of **Maldon**
Given at the GENERAL REGISTER OFFICE, under the Seal of the said Office, the      30th      day of      April      2010

MXE 891615

# Wife freed from death sentence as a "traitor"

### Daily Express Staff Reporter

ALONE, for four hours yesterday, in a court from which all others were excluded, a man sat listening to what are called legal arguments. In the dock, his wife. Dorothy Pamela O'Grady.

And when the arguments were over and the court was "open" again, he heard pronounced words that freed his wife from sentence of death as a traitor, but still kept her from him.

He heard the Lord Chief Justice, Lord Caldecote, say:—

"The conviction on the two capital charges under the Treachery Act has been quashed, and sentence has been passed by the court on charges on which the appellant was convicted, but on which the judge passed no sentence.

"This court has passed a sentence of fourteen years' penal servitude on the counts other than those under the Treachery Act."

The appeal—in the Court of Criminal Appeal—of the only British woman in this war so far to be condemned to death for treachery was over.

Vincent Henry O'Grady reflected: "After her trial they branded her a traitor. She is free from that stigma today, thank God. A great weight is lifted off my mind now. But fourteen years——"

### Talked to him

She was allowed to talk to him when the two wardresses led her from the dock, just as he had been allowed to stay in court after it had been decided that the hearing should be in camera.

He had given an undertaking not to divulge any information.

She is forty-two—"a wonderful wife for fifteen years"; he, twenty years older, left their home at Sandown, Isle of Wight, when the London blitz began to return to his old job of fighting fires.

Now, with the two wardresses sitting a little way from them, cups of tea before them, they talked—and wept.

Outside was a prison car waiting to drive Mrs. O'Grady away.

More than half an hour passed. Then one of the wardresses tapped the plump, bespectacled little woman on the shoulder. "I'm sorry—time to go," she whispered.

"Well, Vin, this is the last time you'll kiss me," Mrs. O'Grady murmured. "Promise me one thing—don't let any one else have my dog. I'd rather you had Rob put to sleep. It would make me happy if you did."

MR. V. H. O'GRADY
Tea together.

"That's all right, my girl—it shall be done," Mr. O'Grady said. But he knew that Rob had already been "put to sleep." He said to me afterwards: "She had left her meat coupons with the butcher so that her dog might have his meals. Every letter from prison was devoted to Rob's welfare."

Husband and wife had each been surprised to find the other in court. "My head is so bad—I don't think I can face it all again," Mrs. O'Grady had written from Holloway.

"I shouldn't come up if I were you," she advised her husband. "Who will look after Rob when you're away? There'd be no one to save him if the house was bombed."

She had added this, too: "Don't trouble to dig up the garden. The 500 bulbs I planted last autumn will come up again."

Mrs. O'Grady was sentenced by Mr. Justice Macnaghten at Hampshire Assizes, Winchester, on December 17.

She was found guilty of two charges under the Treachery Act:—

1—That in the Isle of Wight she made a plan likely to give assistance to the military operations of the enemy.

2—That with intent to help the enemy she committed an act designed to impede the military operations of H.M. Forces by cutting a military telephone wire.

Under the Official Secrets Act she was found guilty of approaching a prohibited place and of possessing a document containing information purporting to be information of defence measures.

She was acquitted on charges of conspiring with persons unknown and of endeavouring to force a safeguard.

Few pictures survive of Vincent O'Grady. This press image was taken in February 1941 when he attended his wife's successful appeal against the convictions under the Treachery Act, which had threatened to see her hang as a traitor. (*Daily Express*)

Pictured in 2011, this spacious house on the hilly southern fringe of Sandown is Osborne Villa, O'Grady's guest house home at the time of her arrest in 1940. She returned to the villa after her release from prison in 1950, remaining there until 1963. (Matt Searle)

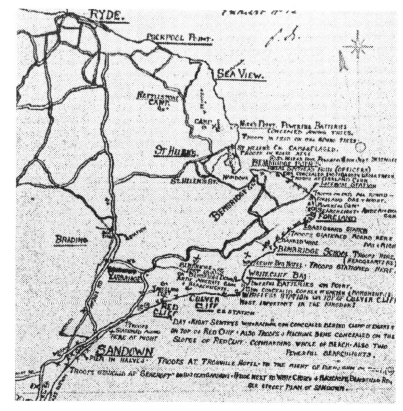

Extract from Dorothy O'Grady's detailed map of the Isle of Wight's eastern coastline in 1940, concentrating on the defences in and around Sandown Bay, an area initially earmarked for invasion by Germany. While it contains some inaccuracies, the comprehension information would certainly have aided the enemy. (The National Archives)

This official War Office photograph was taken at Culver Down Battery on 24 August 1940 at the very time O'Grady was compiling maps and drawing sketches of the Isle of Wight's coastal defences. Royal Artillery gun crews are pictured taking up positions at the battery's 9.2in guns during a practice shoot. (Imperial War Museum)

Another War Office photograph, taken on 7 August 1941, depicts gunners rushing to their posts on th 9.2in weapons at the north-facing Needles (New) Battery. A year earlier, O'Grady had been well place while 'on the run' at Totland to spy on the battery, and several other defensive sites in the island's far wes (Imperial War Museum)

Early twentieth-century view of HMP Aylesbury, where O'Grady was twice jailed: initially as a young woman, when she was sent there for Borstal training; then between 1941 and 1950, when she was imprisoned for her string of wartime crimes. (Author's collection)

Close to the spot where Dorothy O'Grady was arrested by the army in 1940, this newly erected section of barrier guarded the beach at Yaverland from an enemy landing. Such obstacles would have been an increasingly familiar sight for O'Grady as, repeatedly, she trespassed with her dog on the zoned-off foreshore. (Author's collection)

Culver Down Battery's 9.2in guns were an important component in the wartime defence of the Isle of Wight and the eastern approach to the Solent. O'Grady noted their presence on her illicit maps. The emplacements survive today, in the care of the National Trust, as an evocative reminder of the island's military past. This 2011 photograph was taken looking south towards Sandown Bay. (Matt Searle)

Fort Bembridge, high on Bembridge Down, is the most complete of the surviving wartime military sites in the area of Dorothy O'Grady's arrest by the army in 1940. Photographed in 2012, the hexagonal fort, co-ordinating point for the coastal batteries at Culver Down and Nodes Point in wartime, was relinquished by the MOD in 1948 and is now in the care of the National Trust, partly used for light industry, although work to restore original features is under way. (Matt Searle)

Nearest of the four nineteenth-century Solent sea forts to the Isle of Wight was St Helens, pictured here in 2012 from the shoreline. O'Grady's post-war interviews indicate that she was keeping an eye on the fort in 1940. Its principal wartime uses were as a location for searchlight and anti-aircraft defence. (Matt Searle)

This 2011 view of Sandown Bay was taken looking south from the Redcliff area on the lower slopes of the downland, which culminates at Culver Cliff. It was here O'Grady was exercising her dog in August 1940 immediately before she was found by soldiers – not for the first time – on the zoned-off beach below. (Matt Searle)

Vera Schalburg (Erikson), photographed soon after her arrest with two male colleagues in the wake of their disastrous 1940 spying mission to the UK. 'Turned' by MI5, she may have been used to spy on O'Grady in jail and seems to have been allowed to stay in England after the war – possibly in the Isle of Wight. (The National Archives)

The final image of Dorothy O'Grady. Aged 83, she was photographed in 1981, four years before her death, while living in sheltered housing at Lake, Isle of Wight. (Author's collection)

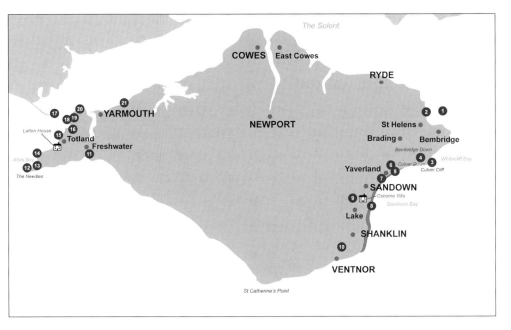

The Isle of Wight in 1940, showing Dorothy O'Grady's close proximity to military installations.
(Sarah Searle)

East

1. St Helens (Sea) Fort – searchlights.
2. Nodes Fort & Battery – heavy gun battery / artillery barracks.
3. Culver Fort & Culver Down Battery – heavy gun battery.
4. Fort Bembridge – artillery barracks / battery observation post / Army radar.
5. (Former) Redcliff Battery – anti-aircraft gun.
6. Yaverland Fort & Battery – searchlights.
7. Sandown (Granite) Fort – pill box; one of many in Sandown Bay area.
8. (Former) Sandown Barracks Battery – disused; guarded.
9. Sandown Barracks – infantry barracks.
10. RAF Ventnor – major radar station.
House icon – O'Grady's home at Osborne Villa, Sandown.

West

11. (Former) Freshwater Redoubt – disused; guarded.
12. Needles (Old) Battery – anti-aircraft gun.
13. Needles (New) Battery – heavy gun battery.
14. (Former) Hatherwood Point Battery – Navy indicator loop.
15. (Former) Warden Point Battery – searchlights / anti-aircraft guns.
16. Golden Hill Fort – infantry depot.
17. Hurst Castle – medium gun battery / searchlights.
18. Fort Albert – medium gun battery.
19. Cliff End Battery – medium gun battery.
20. Fort Victoria – ancillary marine uses.
21. Bouldnor Battery – heavy gun battery / anti-submarine boom / minefield.
House icon – Latton House, Totland (O'Grady arrest site).

Note – Only the more prominent coastal military locations are shown on the map.

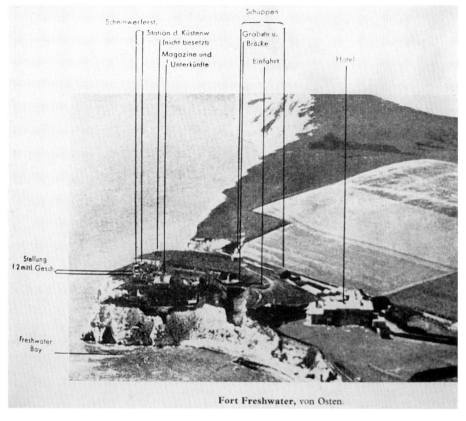

Scheinwerferst.

Schuppen

Station d. Küstenw
(nicht besetzt)

Magazine und
Unterkünfte

Graben u.
Brücke

Einfahrt

Hotel

Stellung
f. 2 mittl. Gesch.

Freshwater
Bay

**Fort Freshwater, von Osten.**

The German armed forces were well briefed on the Isle of Wight's coastline in 1940. This aerial photograph, one of many taken from the skies above the island by the enemy, focusses on *Fort Freshwater von Osten* – Freshwater Fort (Redoubt) from the East. (Author's collection)

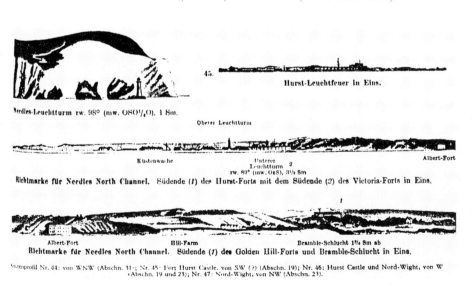

45.

Hurst-Leuchtfeuer in Eins.

Needles-Leuchtturm rw. 98° (mw. OSO¹/₄O), 1 Sm.

Oberer Leuchtturm

Küstenwache

Unterer
Leuchtturm 2
rw. 89° (mw. OzS), 3¹/₂ Sm

Albert-Fort

**Richtmarke für Needles North Channel. Südende (1) des Hurst-Forts mit dem Südende (2) des Victoria-Forts in Eins.**

Albert-Fort

Hill-Farm

Bramble-Schlucht 1³/₄ Sm ab

**Richtmarke für Needles North Channel. Südende (1) des Golden Hill-Forts und Bramble-Schlucht in Eins.**

Küstenprofil Nr. 44: von WNW (Abschn. 31); Nr. 45: Fort Hurst Castle. von SW (?) (Abschn. 19); Nr. 46: Hurst Castle und Nord-Wight, von W (Abschn. 19 und 23); Nr. 47: Nord-Wight, von NW (Abschn. 23).

Hand-drawn coastal profiles were another product of German intelligence. This example, drawing attention to military sites, shows the Isle of Wight's far west, culminating in The Needles, and the adjacent Hampshire coast around Hurst Castle. (Author's collection)

German intelligence also adapted Ordnance Survey maps for identifying coastal features and defensive positions. Sandown Bay, earmarked for a landing in 1940, was among key sections of the Isle of Wight's coast targeted in this process. (Author's collection)

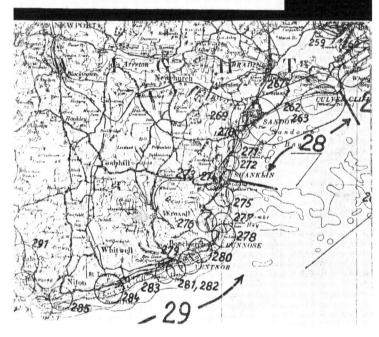

28. **Von Culver Cliff bis Shanklin.** (Karten 34 und 35)

K: Vom Südende der Whitecliff Bay bis Westende des Culver Cliffs Felsklippen mit Steilküste des Culvers Cliffs. Von Yaverland bis Shanklin Flachküste von sandig-kiesiger Beschaffenheit.

S: Weitgehend mit Geröllen bedeckter Strand.

H: Langsam ansteigendes, welliges, nur wenig bewaldetes Hinterland mit vereinzelten, stärker hervortretenden Hügeln. Hart an der Küste die Stadt Sandown. Entlang der Küste zwischen Sandown und Shanklin Eisenbahnlinie und Autostraße (Newport—Wroxall).

29. **Von Shanklin bis Chale** (Karte 35).

K: Gegliederte Steilküste mit niedrigem Kreidekliff, unter 30 bis 35° ansteigende, mit niederem Baumwerk bestandene Verbindungszone („Undercliff") zum oberen Küstenplateau, das sich vorwiegend aus greller Schreibkreide und Grünsanden aufbaut.

S: Schmaler, mit Geröllen bedeckter Strand vor dem Kliff.

H: Unbewaldetes Tafelland mit Straßen- und Eisenbahnen entlang der Küste von Bonchurch nach Niton und Chale.

Photographed from Shanklin soon after the war, Sandown Bay is shown with the anti-invasion barrier erected in 1940 still in place. The broad sweep of the bay, selected at one stage for a German landing, culminates at Culver Cliff (top right). (Author's collection)

O'Grady made notes on troop movements on her illicit 1940 maps. Conspicuous among these was the use of bicycles by soldiers of the 6th Black Watch, part of the British Army's infantry brigade charged with firming up the Isle of Wight's anti-invasion defences. (Imperial War Museum)

A soldier stands guard beneath the barrel of one of the 9.2in guns at Needles (New) Battery in the summer of 1941. The presence of the guns would have been noted by O'Grady when, a year earlier, she was hiding out in nearby Totland. (Imperial War Museum)

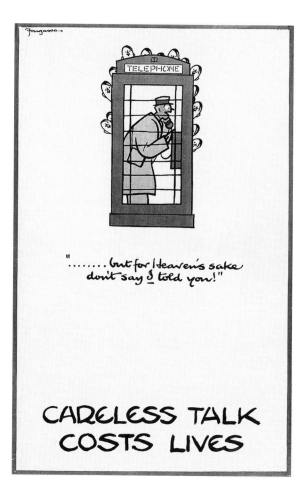

The Ministry of Information underlined the importance of 'careless talk' in its now famous 1940 poster campaign. Dorothy O'Grady paid little, if any, heed to it. (Imperial War Museum)

Among the most sensitive of the Isle of Wight's wartime installations targeted by O'Grady during her intelligence-gathering spree in 1940 was the top-secret RAF Ventnor radar station on St Boniface Down. This declassified site diagram demonstrates the area and extent of the radar station – twice attacked by the Luftwaffe. (Author's collection)

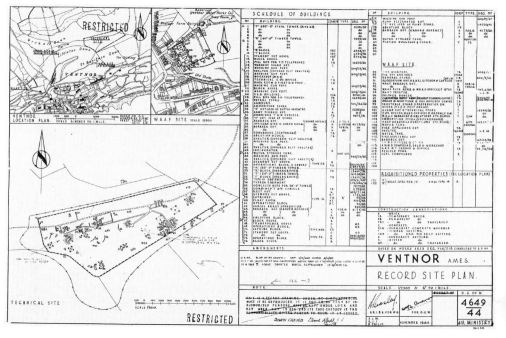

The picturesque remains of St Helens medieval Duver church was among the prominent coastal features noted by O'Grady on her maps. More relevant in the context of her spying mission was the pill box emplacement to the right of the tower and the offshore sea fort seen in the distance. (Sarah Searle)

Still serving in 2012 as a guest house, Latton House at Totland Bay was the scene of O'Grady's recapture by the police in September 1940. (Matt Searle)

Close to O'Grady's Totland hide-out, The Needles headland in 1940 was an especially sensitive military area, supporting two of the batteries guarding the western approach to the Solent. (Matt Searle)

Convent of Notre Dame, Clapham Common, seen here on a postcard from the early part of the twentieth century. It was here the young Dorothy O'Grady almost certainly received her truncated convent schooling. (Author's collection)

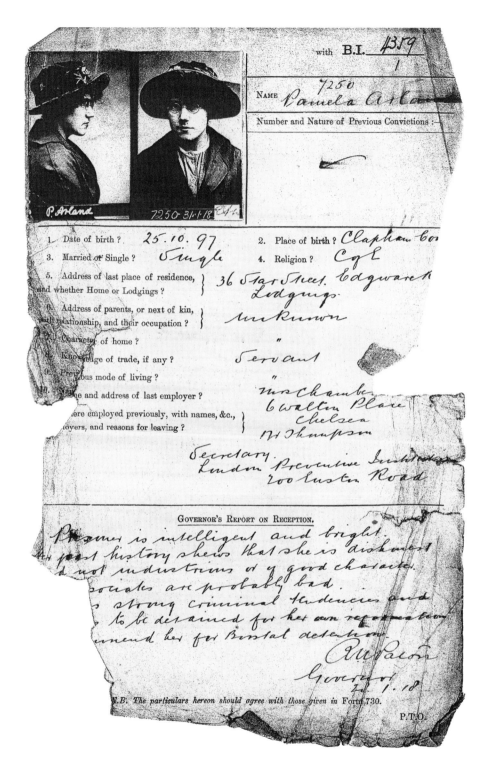

Dorothy O'Grady's criminal career began when she was convicted (as Pamela Arland) in January 1918 of forging banknotes. Partially disintegrated, this archived document includes her initial prison photographs and an assessment by the governor of Holloway prison, in which the young woman is described as 'intelligent and bright' but 'not of good character'. (The National Archives)

the advancing armies, the little German swastika she had inadvertently brushed against.

Speaking to another reporter on the swastika incident, she made the inarguably fair point: 'As if spies went around with their national flags pinned to their coats!' As for her supposedly nocturnal contact with a man from a U-boar, she chortled, 'It would have been virtually impossible for a submarine to do that because of all the precautions.' And her professed admiration for Adolf Hitler? 'Really, I hated him,' said Dorothy. 'But,' she added, 'everyone listened to me.'

She repeated her regret at not being able to speak at her trial, insisting again that she really had wanted to tell the truth in court – despite the thrill of being tried for her life – and put the record straight on one thing in particular. 'I certainly wanted to deny cutting telephone lines because I never ever did that,' she said. Yet, true to form, she reiterated that this regret was, at the least, matched at the time by her disappointment at the specifics of the 'death by hanging' sentence. 'In all the books I had read, spies were shot,' added Dorothy ruefully.

It must have seemed to this latest batch of bemused interviewers as unreal as it had to Rodin, Hill and the other journalists she had entertained – and baffled – years earlier. 'I felt it wasn't really happening and it was tremendously interesting,' said Dorothy in her apparently crystal-clear recall of the moment the sentence was passed. 'I had always wanted to see it done in real life instead of watching it on films.' Clearly, being condemned to death at the hands of the hangman, instead of by a firing squad, was not a wholly displeasing option for her.

And, as Sidney Rodin had reported in 1950, neither, in the end, was the eventual post-appeal sentence of imprisonment. For the woman who, despite her professed disappointment at not being able to reveal the truth at her trial, would apparently have welcomed some sort of inverted martyrdom courtesy of the State Executioner, the years in Aylesbury jail had actually proved a perfectly adequate consolation prize. She had been able to hang on to her 'importance' within the confines of the prison. 'It was certainly a fascinating experience,' she said.

Fascinating new copy for the reporters was provided by Dorothy's recall of women with whom she had served her time at Aylesbury. 'Two Irish girls were imprisoned there for some sort of bombing. Such nice girls. I could hardly believe they were capable of doing that.' Possibly of greater interest was her memory of 'a Russian countess who had a picture of herself in robes and coronet, but was so haughty-taughty that she never spoke to me, so we never knew why she was there'. Dorothy also remembered 'a German girl' who was incarcerated at the prison 'to be kept under observation' and a woman convicted for posting leaflets through people's letterboxes, 'saying Hitler was right'.

Dorothy, of course, had said much the same thing herself – and it seemed clear in 1981 that her most treasured memories of her nine years at Aylesbury were of her own status. 'I was quite a personality there because they looked up to me, thinking I was a real spy. It was great to be thought clever and intelligent,' she said.

Basking in her own invented glory, she could relax and even enjoy the mundane aspects of prison life – 'I liked mending uniforms for the Borstal girls who were living nearby' – but there had been one unpleasant incident. 'The only bad thing was when a member of staff's relative died in the war and she took it out on me, wrecking my room and taking my nice handkerchiefs, but I didn't hold it against her. It was understandable because she thought I was a real spy.'

Dorothy gave every indication that the passing decades had not diminished her delight at outwitting Britain's wartime establishment. Recalling MI5's attempts, soon after her arrival in jail, to prise from her the names of agents she had worked for or with – 'it's just me, no-one else,' she told the officer who came to interrogate her. She added in her *Weekly Post* interview:

> I had a chuckle because he thought he was so clever and there was I, pulling his leg, and he didn't realise it! ... believe me, I was really proud of the fact that I had fooled the clever officers – with all their education – as well as the police and the courts. They had all proved how they could be taken in by a simple woman.

But hadn't *she* been incredibly stupid to have endured such an ordeal as nine years in prison – after narrowly escaping execution – all for the sake of a fantasy and a bit of a giggle? Dorothy didn't see it that way. 'It wasn't an ordeal because I enjoyed it and I think I would do the same again now if I were younger.'

Nonetheless, if she was speaking the truth in 1981, and had been doing so since 1950, her behaviour in wartime had clearly not been that of a normally functioning human being. Just as she had told Sidney Rodin, and in much the same terms, Dorothy admitted as much in most of these final interviews with the press.

'Looking back, I realise I must have been suffering from a sort of kink. What I did in wartime was stupid and I brought the punishment on myself. I know people will always think of me as a spy, but I never was,' she reflected solemnly. 'I was just a very silly woman who got the punishment she deserved.'

Her reference again to a probable 'kink' in her character seemed as much an understatement in the 1980s as it had been in that initial interview with the *Sunday Express*. But if her actions in 1940 had been influenced by psychological abnormality, this would surely have been discovered and acted upon either before or after her conviction and sentencing – fifth column scare culture or not. Yet, according to Dorothy, she was never examined by a psychiatrist.

'A telling fact,' the *Weekly Post* duly noted, 'Perhaps a trained mind could have penetrated to the heart of the matter, particularly on studying Dorothy's past.'

So the *Post*, along with Dorothy's other 1981 interviewers at Porter Court, ventured down the path, previously trodden by Sidney Rodin and Peter Hill, as far as possible into Dorothy O'Grady's early life, in the quest to find what may have bred 'the desire to leap out of drudgery into adventure – of whatever kind'.

Collectively, the journalists confirmed that she was the daughter of a British Museum official and revealed that she had attended boarding school, leaving prematurely because of financial pressures. Her mother had died at that time, shattering her world, and the pain, according to Dorothy, was increased when her father married the housekeeper, whom she resented. 'My world ended when my mother died,' she told reporters, 'and from that moment on I did not fear dying myself. That's why I wasn't scared when I was sentenced to death.'

Condemned to years in domestic service, Dorothy told of finding it all a drudge. Recalling how, aged 29, she had married Vincent O'Grady (twenty years her senior, said Dorothy, still apparently under the impression that her husband had been nearly two years older than he actually was), she added that he was not someone given to displays of affection, a man who had refused to let her have children. Without him, however, at the start of the war, she felt alone – and terrified by the shells whizzing over her house. She had taken refuge in her love of animals, in particular the deep affection she felt for Rob, her pet retriever, who was with her that fateful day when she was apprehended on the beach at Yaverland. Under suspicion, she explained, she seized the opportunity of putting an end to the drudgery, the loneliness, the fear. She would become 'a spy'.

The media exposure in 1981 secured for Dorothy the reputation of a woman seriously troubled by the misfortunes of life who had gone to extraordinary lengths to improve her lot. The reaction was largely sympathetic. She had been harmless, an innocent, child-like victim of her own fantasies and probable mental instability. 'Dotty Dorothy' was just about the harshest phrase people would use when they referred to her now, the spy who never was – but wanted to be.

Her 'giggle' at the nation's expense was the story Dorothy O'Grady took to her grave. Her failing health finally had dictated a move from her Porter Court flatlet to the nearby Tower House nursing home in Lake Hill. She died there, two weeks short of her eighty-eighth birthday, on 11 October 1985, from chronic heart disease (coronary occlusion caused by atherosclerosis – hardening of the arteries). Naturally, the local press reported her passing, recalling her many interviews, reinforcing her 'dotty but harmless' reputation. 'She was a very nice old lady who was always very grateful and appreciative,' Dennis Parker, the warden at Porter Court, told the *Isle of Wight County*

*Press*. 'However small the service we rendered her, she always said "thank you" ...' It wasn't a bad epitaph.

Others would look back on her final years a little less charitably. Evidently, some hostility towards her had lingered. Recalling meeting Dorothy at Porter Court, Betty Vine told years later how residents at the complex used to ask, 'How did she manage to get a council place when other people couldn't get into one? And how, when not having much money, did she earlier manage to buy a house in the Broadway outside Sandown Barracks?' Even today, there are some who still harbour suspicions that Osborne Villa may have been purchased for Dorothy by Nazi Germany to serve as a convenient base for her spying activity.

Her death did not spell the end of curiosity and conjecture. Quite the opposite. Dorothy would no doubt have chuckled anew, had she been able, when James Friel used her self-proclaimed adventure story, down to its Sandown backdrop, as the basis for his entertaining novel *Careless Talk* in 1992. She would certainly have enjoyed, had she been alive to hear it, the portrayal of herself by such an acclaimed actress as Maureen Lipman in the BBC Radio 4 play, *The Spy Who Never Was*, two years later. Her story was not only standing the test of time, it seemed to have the legs to run and run, carrying her impish infamy before it.[7]

But then, in 1995, a decade after her death, it was to be dramatically challenged. Her jovial accounts since 1950 were shown to have been highly selective versions of the facts, verbally edited by Dorothy, with key details forgotten or deliberately omitted. Once again, she was front page news.

## Notes

1  Vincent O'Grady's brush with notoriety, courtesy of his wife, is somewhat overshadowed by the infamy with which his birthplace in Holborn's Red Lion Square has for centuries been linked – as the suggested location for the disposal in a pit of the exhumed and mutilated bodies of Oliver Cromwell

and fellow regicides, John Bradshaw and Henry Ireton, following the English monarchy's restoration in 1660.

2 Born on 15 April 1849, Joseph Benedict O'Grady, Vincent's father, had trained as a boy seaman with the Royal Navy between 1864 and 1867, when he signed up for ten years' service. However, while his service record shows that his character was deemed 'very good' and he had no apparent health problems, Joseph remained at sea for little more than a year aboard the ageing former third-rater HMS *Agincourt*. She had been relegated to harbour duties the year he joined her crew. A small man, just 4ft 11in tall, with a ruddy complexion, Joseph appears to have left the Royal Navy on 26 April 1869, apparently preferring life ashore as a Metropolitan Police constable. He later worked as a print compositor.

3 It seems that Dorothy had previous experience of running boarding houses prior to the couple's 1933 move to the island. There are references in the archives to her 'keeping various guest houses' before taken over at Osborne Villa.

4 The fire brigade's Pension Act of 1925 allowed firefighters to retire with a pension equivalent to half their pay providing they had completed twenty-five years' service and had reached the age of 55. Vincent O'Grady's fifty-fifth birthday was in December 1933, yet (along with Dorothy and Agnes O'Grady) he is listed on the Isle of Wight's Register of Electors as living at Osborne Villa in Sandown the previous October. It seems he was permitted to terminate his London Fire Brigade employment a few months early.

5 Following her husband's death, Dorothy's fellow residents at Osborne Villa were mainly single people – Harold Symonds, for example, lived there for the best part of a decade from 1954 – but the house also counted one married couple, William and Frances Jones, among its occupants in the mid-1950s.

6 Shanklin Cottage Hospital closed in 1990.

7 Friel, James, *Careless Talk* (London: Macmillan, 1992).

# 8

# A Most Dangerous and Cunning Spy

The year 1995 stands out in the political career of Barry Field, the Isle of Wight's MP since the General Election of June 1987. It was the year the 48-year-old Conservative backbencher announced his candidature for the Tory leadership in the wake of Prime Minister John Major's challenging ('put up or shut up') midsummer resignation from the post. While vehemently denying he was either a 'stalking horse' or a 'seaside donkey' – both of which he had been dubbed by unsympathetic opponents and media – Field later withdrew from the contest when John Redwood quit his job as Welsh Secretary to lead the ultimately doomed right wing bid to oust Major from the helm of the party. The Isle of Wight MP's brief exposure to the glare of the national spotlight quickly faded.

This was not, however, the first time that Barry Field had helped to make front page news in 1995. In the May of that year, just weeks before John Major ignited the summer's political furore, the MP had played a key role in fanning – into a veritable blaze of outright media-fired rejection – the flames of renewed doubt about the legacy of Dorothy O'Grady as the eccentric yet, in the eyes of many, endearing spy who never was. At the end of it all, her reputation lay in shreds.

She was exposed and widely convicted afresh as the spy who *always* was – an assessment that, in many quarters, has endured to this day. It was an ironic twist given Barry Field's original, laudable, intention of delivering to O'Grady posthumous official recognition of her harmless status. A realistic aim it had seemed.

The problem for the MP in trying to clear Dorothy's name was the almost complete lack of formal evidence or explanation on which to base his case. The testimony from her trial and earlier court hearings in 1940 had been given in secret. Nothing had been published at the time or since apart from the bare outline of the legal process used to convict her. The only account made public which purported to be the full story was that given in interview by O'Grady herself.

It might have been substantially believed but it hardly amounted to an impartial version of events. The documents Barry Field needed in order to pursue his quest, the trial records from 1940, had remained locked away from public view and, while their 'closed' status in the mid-1990s had been the subject of an official review, their release as de-classified open documents had not been expected until well into the twenty-first century. In fact, events had overtaken this widely held assumption. The Crown Prosecution Service's records office had published its review in the July 1994 issue of the *CPS Journal*. As a result, the O'Grady file had very soon afterwards been formally declared as 'open' and released to the Public Records Office at Kew, available for inspection by the public.

Its release had passed largely unnoticed by those with an interest in the case and it was to the Isle of Wight MP's credit that, in May 1995, he was told by the Home Office that the elusive papers it contained were readily accessible to him. Through his prompting, he was able to bring to the attention of the public key information about Dorothy that might otherwise have been initially missed by people who, like myself, had temporarily taken their eye off the O'Grady 'ball'.

Barry Field enlisted the help of local news agency journalist Mike Merritt to spread the word on the long-sought evidence he hoped would finally endorse O'Grady's self-crafted 'dotty Dorothy' image and rid her – and the island on which she had for so long lived – of any lingering association with the Third Reich.

The enterprising Merritt did a good job – but the story he sold to a clutch of national news desks was dramatically different from the one anticipated by the MP. 'I set out to clear her name but I am staggered by the treachery she sunk to. She could have altered the direction of the war,' Field was widely quoted as saying the day the story broke. The MP's denunciation of Dorothy was emphatic: 'Far from being a simple seaside landlady, she was a highly skilled agent. The German jackboot could have been stamped on Britain as a result of what she did.'

The O'Grady saga was once again a sensation, picked up and carried in a media whirlwind by broadsheets and tabloids alike, with TV and radio galloping in for their share of the spoils. What had Field and Merritt discovered that, overnight, had so dramatically changed perceptions about the 'unconventional lady who refused to take the war seriously' – the description applied by *The Times* to Dorothy's widely accepted image prior to the new disclosures? Some sections of the national media were now calling her one of Hitler's most dangerous spies.

Revealed for the first time within the pile of 'new' documents were some missing details from her early life. She had been adopted as a newly born infant in 1897 by British Museum official George Squire and his wife, Pamela, who lived at Clapham Common in south London and provided Dorothy with a convent education for a limited period at the boarding school she had mentioned in her 1981 press interviews. By the time she was 17 both her adoptive parents had died and Dorothy had moved to north-west London where she was employed as a domestic worker at the home of the Rector of Christ Church in Harrow, the Rev. Ruby. While none of this was at odds with O'Grady's own account of her formative years, it added markedly more detail than she had chosen to divulge – and the next part of the story she had totally ignored.

Her tale of leading a life of dull routine before the war was revealed to have been, at the very least, economical with the truth. Routine there had been, but it was not of the sort that most people would define as dull or humdrum. Dorothy O'Grady had routinely been in trouble with the law. She had acquired a criminal record as a young woman which included convictions for theft, forgery and prostitution in the years leading right up to her marriage in August 1926.

Dorothy had been no stranger to prison life when she was sent down in 1941. Whether the years between marriage to the undemonstrative Vincent O'Grady and the outbreak of war had seemed monotonous to her was something of a moot point but, prior to this, she had certainly succeeded in drawing attention to herself – and had later entirely airbrushed her colourful criminal career from the version of her life story she had disclosed to journalists in her many interviews.

The nature of her pre-war crimes was seized upon by the press as a firm pointer to her guilt and treachery in 1940. A woman with proven experience at forging banknotes – her first offence, for which she was sentenced to three years' Borstal training in 1918 – would, it was suggested, seem well-suited to the delicate task of drawing detailed maps and accurate sketches of military installations. And might the seedy streets of London's Soho, where it seemed she had plied her trade as a prostitute – appearing four times before the courts for soliciting offences between 1923 and 1926 – have been the recruiting ground in which her services as a potential German agent were secretly secured? 'She had clearly been turned by Germany at an early age,' said Barry Field.[1]

In fact, there was a more compelling reason for linking the forgery and prostitution offences – which had occurred either side of a conviction in 1920 for stealing clothes as a servant, for which she was sentenced to two years' hard labour – with O'Grady's wartime transgressions. The prosecution papers held another damning revelation. The young Dorothy had more than once been charged under an assumed name when she first came to the attention of the police. She was calling herself Pamela Arland. Pamela was her real second name; the origin of Arland could only be guessed at. The prosecution file showed that, two decades later, when arrested at the Totland guest house in 1940 and found to have been living there under a false name, she had evidently resurrected the same baffling alias. Truly, this was a woman with a double identity.

And, it now appeared, a woman with a grudge – long-felt and sufficiently bitter to persuade her to work against the interests of the United Kingdom in the Second World War. It was a grudge that dated back to her career as a London prostitute.

'In letters written in prison,' reported the *Daily Mail* in its two-page feature on the newly obtained file's revelations:

> O'Grady tells how she waited 16 years to wreak her revenge for the bitterness she felt about being 'wrongly' fined in the 1920s. Her anger was fuelled because her beloved puppy had died while she was on remand. She never forgave the British authorities, and Nazi Germany became the 'allied force' with which to strike back at the Establishment she hated.

A picture of the middle-aged Dorothy, smiling for the camera, looking anything but bitter, illustrated the *Daily Express*'s own feature spread on the 'truth about the landlady who spied for Hitler'. The caption's bold text was ready-made: 'Avenger.' Ironically, this was the same photograph published with Sidney Rodin's 1950 article for the *Sunday Express*, which had told a very different story.

The trial papers substantially confirmed her account of the long walks in the summer of 1940 with the adored Rob, and her frequent presence in forbidden areas, revealing that on 2 August she had been formally cautioned and warned to keep away from the coast after being caught on a Sandown beach with the retriever. It was also regarded as pertinent by the prosecution that, when the army's patience with her finally snapped on Yaverland beach seven days later, O'Grady was found to be engrossed in the contents of an Isle of Wight guidebook.

Also noted in the CPS file was her subsequent attempt to buy her way out of trouble at Yaverland, the finding of her self-drawn maps and sketches of the military's coastal defence measures (those preserved with the trial records seemed impressively detailed and, to a degree, skilfully drawn), her arrest at Totland; and the discovery behind her lapel of the barely concealed swastika badge.

But there was more in those critical papers, further key details which had never previously been made public, information sufficiently weighty to swing the pendulum the other way and expose Dorothy O'Grady for what the media were now virtually unanimous in agreeing she had always been – a mistress of the double bluff. In essence, the press reports compiled from Mike Merritt's copy collectively insisted that she *had* spied for the enemy but had deliberately given the impression, right up to her death, of being a harmless eccentric with a dangerous wartime fantasy – a convenient cover story for her sinister pro-Nazi activity.

A raft of witness statements showed that her attempt at bribery on Yaverland beach was not an isolated incident. She had several times tried to gain access to areas within military zones by offering soldiers chocolates or cigarettes in her endeavours to garner the highly sensitive information she needed for her maps and pencil sketches. Her degree of success was amply demonstrated by the depth of detail she was able to include on her map of the particularly sensitive coastal area around Sandown Bay, a key piece of evidence in the prosecution's case.

While clarity was in places sacrificed for the sheer amount of information she chose to include, the map was, on the face of it, a comprehensive guide to the geography and the military installations in place at that vital period – from the position of gun emplacements and searchlights to the location of barbed wire obstacles; from the presence of troops to the number of soldiers sleeping at a given time; from lorries apparently camouflaged by trees to the steepness of cliffs.

Dorothy, of course, had been perfectly willing in her press interviews to admit to her brazen attempts to obtain militarily sensitive information so that she would hopefully be arrested as a spy. However, the sheer amount of detail she had included on her map of Sandown Bay, coupled with the facts of her long-concealed criminal past and apparent grudge motive for working against the interests of her country, were certainly sufficient to cast serious doubts over her tale.

Whether it was correct to describe what she had drawn as 'terrifyingly accurate' – the verdict on O'Grady's map-making in the *Today* newspaper – was, to put it mildly, an arguable point, but there had clearly been sufficient detail seriously to worry senior military intelligence officers such as Lt. Col. Edward Hinchley Cooke, who was among those to interview Dorothy after her Totland arrest. The trial papers included his conclusion that the information she had gathered 'would be of very great importance to the enemy and is therefore of vital importance as far as the defence of that part of the country is concerned'.

Much was made in some of the 1995 press coverage of O'Grady's apparent awareness of radar on the cliffs at the northern end of the bay. 'Wireless station on top of Culver Cliff. Most important in the kingdom' was the precise wording of the text on her map. This led to one of the less persuasive strands of journalistic interpretation. Dorothy had not actually referred to the term 'radar' at all. Her use instead on the map of 'wireless' was correct, a reference to the Royal Navy's shore signals and wireless station which would have been easily visible on Culver. It wasn't radar but, while calling it the country's most important was hyperbole, noting the station's existence would have been potentially valuable data for the enemy, so its inclusion on the map was significant.[2]

However, according to her own account, Dorothy apparently *had* been aware of the existence of radar elsewhere on the Isle of Wight when snooping around the island's coast – at the RAF facility on St Boniface Down, Ventnor, which she claimed during her press interviews to have visited, noted and sketched in August 1940.

The newly released trial papers exposed O'Grady's protestations that she had never cut military telephone lines as a probable outright lie. The evidence was that, on six occasions in the ten days prior to her Totland arrest in September 1940, she had cut communication lines linking searchlight sites with coastal gun batteries. It was surely inconceivable that Dorothy could have forgotten that.

Her smiling face from a picture taken in 1981 beamed incongruously beneath the *Daily Mail's* strident headline, 'Dotty Dorothy, Nazi spy'.

The story she had taken to the grave was falling apart. 'Not only was she indeed a Nazi spy, she was one of the most dangerous and cunning they ever recruited – and might have given the Germans a vital foothold on British soil,' the *Mail* informed its readers.

The article told how 'in remarkably frank interviews following her arrest' O'Grady had 'made admissions to which she never subsequently referred publicly. She disclosed that she had lived with a Dutchman before the war and said that a Dutch friend had been hanged at Pentonville prison.' The *Mail* added correctly that, of the sixteen wartime spies executed in Britain, two were indeed Dutch – Carl Meier and Charles van den Kieboom, hanged at Pentonville in December 1940, the first to suffer execution under the new Treachery Act (see Chapter 4). 'It is unlikely that O'Grady was fantasising as these two executions were not widely reported at the time,' the *Mail's* report asserted.

This was another of the less convincing aspects of the press coverage. In fact, there is no corroborating evidence to link O'Grady directly with either of the Dutch spies – apart from the coinciding period of their respective offences in 1940 – and the executions of the two men were reported in the British press at the time. While the lack of supportive evidence does not, in itself, conclusively preclude the possibility that Dorothy was in some way allied to the Dutchmen, it is – and was in 1995 – highly unlikely. But then, if she truly had been a spy, it could conceivably be argued that her reference to this was a smokescreen. Spies lie.

What MI5 made of it was not disclosed – and neither was the Security Service's reaction to an extraordinary series of events which, the 'new' documents revealed, had taken place while Dorothy was awaiting trial in Holloway. 'O'Grady was caught trying to signal to German bombers during an air raid, befriending a Russian suspected of being a spy, and handing out swastikas to inmates,' the *Mail's* report continued. The implication clearly was that these were the actions of a highly committed agent prepared to go to any lengths to serve her Nazi employers – rather than those of a dangerously disturbed fantasist.

'During her prison sentence,' reported *The Times* in apparent confirmation, 'she befriended a warder and insisted that her loyalties were with the Third Reich.'

This, the *Daily Mail* contended, was further borne out by the contents of unpublished interviews and letters in which Dorothy was 'clear-headed and honest about her motives'. She had talked of making plans for 'a man on the mainland' and of being part of a ring of four spies whose names she never knew. And, added the *Mail*'s report, 'in a rare prison letter to her husband she asks if anybody else has been caught ... a possible reference to Rose Murphy, an Isle of Wight woman jailed for signalling Morse code messages to German planes.'

Stories had circulated for some time on the island about the alleged espionage and subsequent imprisonment of a Rose Murphy, with Bembridge Down usually given as the location for her suggested flashing of coded signals to the Luftwaffe. Research has revealed no firm evidence to support this, though the rumours persist. The National Archives has no record of anyone of that name being convicted of any form of espionage activity during the war. Possibly there has been confusion between the Irish-sounding surnames of O'Grady and Murphy.[3]

Dorothy's reaction to her own capture at Totland on 10 September 1940 was, it seemed from the prosecution papers, one of outrageous bravado. The *Daily Mail* reported that she had told the police officers who arrested her that, when the invaders came, they 'should be wiped out' – it wasn't clear whether she was referring to the officers specifically or the British nation as a whole – and Germany would 'please herself when she started it'. The assumption was that the Sandown landlady knew as much as anyone in Britain at the time about the enemy's plans for invading England's south coast. She had enthusiastically, methodically and significantly spent the summer of 1940 helping to prepare the ground.

However, despite her bravado, she had it seemed concluded that the game was up for her when she was caught in the Totland guest house. One of the most dramatic revelations to emerge from the 'new' evidence was that, while she was being taken by car to the police station at Yarmouth, she tried to swallow twenty tablets containing the stimulant drug ephedrine hydrochloride from a bottle she was carrying in an apparent attempt to commit suicide – an outcome thwarted by prompt action on the part of the accompanying policemen to prevent ingestion. A photograph of the bottle of 'suicide pills' was among the pictorial evidence preserved in the Crown files – and prominently reproduced in the press. The incident itself was yet another key piece of the story 'airbrushed' by O'Grady.[4]

She could not, however, be similarly accused about another previously undisclosed facet, one which surely would have been a feature of her gleeful story-telling had she known of it. The trial papers revealed that the Director of Public Prosecutions in wartime, Sir Edward Tindal Atkinson, was so determined that Dorothy should hang for her crimes that he had written on 17 January 1941 – as she awaited her appeal hearing – what *Today* correctly called 'a highly irregular' confidential note to Sir Ernley Blackwell at the Home Office.

'I think that the sentence of death ought to go forward,' he told the Acting Chief Justice and former chief legal adviser to the Cabinet. 'If this woman is reprieved, the knowledge of her reprieve would go not only to the public, but would also go to the German intelligence service, and in both these aspects it can well be counted that a reprieve would serve as encouragement to female spies.'[5, 6]

While it was possible to understand Atkinson's desire for O'Grady's execution to serve as a deterrent to other British women tempted to spy for the enemy, it was harder to believe that the DPP would so strongly have advocated her death without truly believing she had posed a genuine, deliberate threat to national security.

Following her arrest in Totland, the trial papers showed, Dorothy was asked by police, 'Did you consider you were assisting this country by committing these acts?'

'Who wants to?' she replied.

It was compelling stuff for the media – and certainly for someone with a fascination for the O'Grady case which stretched back more than a decade. Knowing of my interest as a journalist and author in Dorothy, Mike Merritt had asked for my input in preparing his story. I had provided him with some of the background detail which was to form part of the extensive national press coverage.

When he told me what he had discovered from his read-through of the Crown's 1940 prosecution documents I was persuaded that he and Barry Field had indeed unravelled the probable truth about this stranger-than-fiction wartime episode. Clearly, there was a lot more to Mrs O'Grady than she had wanted anyone to know, or had told them, about while she was alive – that pre-war criminal career and its apparently sinister implications, the grudge she bore against Britain that seemed to have triggered a possible motive for her wartime treachery, the sheer intensity, degree and methodology of her spying activity on the Isle of Wight in the summer of 1940 and the apparent suicide attempt in the police car. Her espionage methods may have lacked orthodoxy but it did now seem possible that at some level she had aligned herself with the Nazi German cause.

The press reported my verdict: 'I have always had an open mind about her, but with this evidence, particularly the detailed maps which were clearly made by somebody trained in intelligence-gathering, the finger firmly points to the conclusion that she was a spy. It is the jigsaw finally put into place after 54 years.' In the many TV and radio interviews that followed in May 1995 I said much the same thing. No doubt about it – Dorothy O'Grady had been nailed as a traitor.

On reflection, I should have been more cautious. There had been a notable exception to the otherwise blanket condemnation of Dorothy as a spy among the five national newspapers which snapped up Mike Merritt's copy. The *Daily Telegraph* may have topped its virtual full page coverage of the new revelations with the lilting headline, 'Landlady who liked to spy beside the seaside.' but journalist Ben Fenton's introductory paragraph was markedly more circumspect in its approach.

'Details of the trial of perhaps the oddest spy of the Second World War have been released 54 years after she was sentenced to hang,' he wrote. 'But the question remains: was Dorothy O'Grady a cunning

Nazi agent or a seaside landlady with a dangerous fantasy?' Fenton had been speaking with someone who had obviously influenced his treatment of the story and reinforced his doubts.

Having quoted my own reaction, he had followed it with a tailpiece comment from Professor Sir Harry Hinsley, a noted authority on the history of British intelligence. Sir Harry did not think it likely that O'Grady had been part of a Nazi ring. He advised against drawing conclusions from the fact that the DPP wanted her hanged. 'They were very keen to kill anybody they could that smacked of helping the enemy – flashing lights at bombers, or whatever,' he said.[7]

However, the general press view of O'Grady's treachery prevailed and there has really been very little published or broadcast since then in the mainstream media to seriously undermine it. In May 1995 there was no longer any doubt that she had committed the crimes for which she was imprisoned in 1941, escaping execution by a legal hair's breadth, but the nagging question remained – did that really equate to sufficient proof that she had been a wartime enemy agent?

Barry Field certainly had no doubts about O'Grady's apparent unmasking as a traitor, Mike Merritt sincerely believed it too, convinced by the strength of the evidence against her, and had made a tidy sum of money from selling the story along those lines. And, with the noted exception of the *Daily Telegraph*, Fleet Street had largely bought it – in every sense of the phrase – lock, stock and barrel. But it has never been as black and white as that in the saga of Dorothy O'Grady. Had we all been too accepting of this dramatic new twist in Dorothy's tale?

It was not long before resurfacing doubts were reinforced by the response to the Merritt revelations of two journalists whose words carried the authority of first-hand encounters with the woman at the centre of the story. 'She was never a spy, just a silly woman who liked telling stories,' insisted George Chastney, a seasoned Isle of Wight-based reporter with the *Southern Evening Echo* who had interviewed O'Grady a decade earlier and remained entirely unconvinced that the release of the documents used to convict her had materially changed anything. Yes, she had done what they said she had, but it was all an elaborate game.[8]

Similarly unimpressed by the new slant on the O'Grady legacy was Peter Hill, who had retained a keen interest in Dorothy's life since interviewing her in 1962 for his televised BBC South account. In 1995, three years after stepping down as the BBC's parliamentary correspondent, Hill fired a broadside at the body of opinion now insisting his former interviewee really had worked for Hitler.

Peter Hill's intervention was uncomfortable for Barry Field. The MP's role in revealing the story of Dorothy's apparent guilt had been significant but his comments on what he now believed to have been her true wartime status – 'a highly skilled agent ... she could have altered the direction of the war' – were perhaps unguarded, a little over-the-top for someone who, as he was rather forced by Hill to concede, had not actually seen any of the documents in question.

Indeed, when Hill's disparaging assessment of the British press' latest take on O'Grady appeared in the *British Journalism Review*'s September 1995 issue, he was able to show, correctly, that the only person apart from Mike Merritt to have inspected the file in the period immediately following its release was himself.

Something of a battle of words ensued, much of it played out in the pages of the *Isle of Wight County Press*, with Hill suggesting that Field, by his forthright comments, had misled the public into believing he had read the trial transcript with its supporting documentation, and the MP retaliating by saying that, while he had been the first individual granted access to the papers since 1940, he denied ever claiming to have actually seen them. 'This chap Hill is miffed because it blows the pieces of work he did right out of the water and for some reason he is out for revenge,' Field told the weekly newspaper's Suzanne Pert.

Dorothy O'Grady's capacity for stirring up a storm of controversy was showing no sign of abating, despite the fact that she had been dead for ten years. Peter Hill was justified in making the point that anyone who had not actually inspected the 'new' evidence at first hand – myself included – should probably have erred on the side of caution when commenting on it. He wrote that three of the national papers who had published the story had confirmed to him that 'they were presented with Merritt's tale one afternoon without foreknowledge, and without having seen the files themselves, although they made their own checks in the time they had.' However, only Ben Fenton's checks had signalled doubt.

In truth, while obviously fascinating for journalists, this was all a bit of a sideshow. What was far more relevant and interesting was Peter Hill's own interpretation of the prosecution papers. What had he discovered in his own read-through? Why did he still scorn the possibility that Dorothy had been a spy?

Wisely, he too had sought out the views of Sir Harry Hinsley, noting in the *BJR* article that 'nowhere in his mammoth *History of British Intelligence in World War II* is she [O'Grady] mentioned'. Added Hill, 'He confirmed to me in writing that it is his opinion – and he stresses that it is only his view – based on the impression he formed after studying the counter-intelligence situation in the UK in 1940, that the Germans had 'no agents in place that were in contact with them before they tried to land about 20 (unsuccessfully) late in the summer.' He also stated in his history that there was no radio traffic from agents at that time.'[9]

Hill quoted from Sir Harry's book: 'In April 1940 similar traffic was intercepted from a station somewhere in Eire, but, apart from those exchanged with 'SNOW' [a turned German agent], no transmission to or from the UK had yet been detected, and it was beginning to be reasonable to assume that no others were being made.' In other words, if Dorothy O'Grady was spying for the enemy, she was not managing to pass on any discernible information to them.[10]

While, in itself, this did not necessarily rule out the possibility that she had been equipped to feed the Germans intelligence by radio, or perhaps by some other means of communication, Peter Hill constructed a powerfully persuasive argument in distancing himself from any such notion. 'At her trial there was no evidence that Mrs O'Grady had a radio set, understood or held codes, had been a member of an extreme organisation like the British Fascists, spoke German, had been abroad, had been recruited or trained, or that she was part of a ring.' He added, correctly, 'Although MI5 tried hard to find out who "Mr Big" was, they failed, Indeed, on the first count at her trial, of conspiracy, she was acquitted.'

Peter Hill harboured little doubt that, while she clearly had edited out unpleasant detail in order to preserve her 'dotty' but, to many, endearing image, Dorothy's much repeated post-war version of events, her 'huge joke', was substantially accurate. She'd done just about everything she could to be suspected of spying, but 'the truth is far more likely to be that ... she made it up'.

The reasons for this strange behaviour 'go deep, back into her past', Hill continued, echoing O'Grady's own account of her troubled early life. He was able to add some potentially illuminating new facts about the unsettling effect on the young Dorothy, when she was just ten years old, of her adoptive mother, Pamela Squire's death and her father's subsequent marriage to the housekeeper, who, explained Hill, 'was cruel to her and pulled her hair'. A year later, the deeply resented stepmother callously told the girl that George and Pamela Squire were not her real parents, that she had been an orphan. 'It was a terrible shock.'

Hill told of Dorothy's overpowering feeling of insignificance and the story-telling she adopted to overcome this and grab attention, aspects of her early life she had admitted to. He detailed her criminal career as a young woman, something she had, of course, kept resolutely quiet about. None of this threw much in the way of new light on her story. But his research had yielded an interesting new facet linked to her final pre-war conviction – for prostitution in 1926.

The prosecution papers revealed that she was sentenced for the offence on 31 July that year. The punishment was a £2 fine or twenty-one days' imprisonment, this being her fourth conviction for soliciting. It was unclear from the records which of the two optional penalties was applied, but if she served the time, her release from jail would have been on 21 August – the very same day she married Vincent O'Grady in Maldon. This sat awkwardly with Peter Hill's assertion, based on Dorothy's letters from Holloway while awaiting her trial, that she had not told Vincent of her past. 'In fact, she was terrified he would find out,' added Hill, convinced that this was key to her subsequent behaviour in wartime.

Offering an entirely new slant on the reason behind Dorothy's flight from justice in August 1940, Hill wrote, 'When she was arrested for being on Sandown beach, and summoned to attend the court, she went on the run, not to avoid detection as a spy, but because she feared the trial would bring out her criminal past, of which she was ashamed, and lose her the one man who cared for her.'

Dorothy, of course, had offered no hint of this in her press interviews, instead giving the impression that she had fled to Totland 'on a whim' to extend her game of spying make-believe, but this now appeared to have been another probable lie. Peter Hill quoted from a letter she had written from prison to her solicitor on 26 November 1940, expressing serious concern about the possibility of references being made at her forthcoming trial to her previous convictions. 'I am more worried over that [the fines for prostitution] than with anything to do with my present case,' she told the lawyer, adding, 'In fact, I cannot think clearly about my present case for worrying about the other matter.'

The four prostitution convictions between 1923 and 1926 carried profound significance for Dorothy in more ways than one. Apart from her professed shame and apparent dread that her husband would find out about this, there was also that 'grudge' she bore against the British authorities for what she claimed had been a wrongful prosecution – one which led to the death of her beloved puppy. What had Peter Hill made of this? Expanding on the details revealed by Mike Merritt, he referred to further pre-trial letters sent by Dorothy from Holloway.

In one, written by Dorothy to her solicitor on 21 November 1940, 'she explained ... that the first conviction for prostitution came about after she was nursing the sick puppy and went out at night in London desperately asking people in the street where a chemist could be found. Arrested for soliciting by the police, she pleaded not guilty and was kept on remand for a week, as was the practice, during which time her dog died. She felt this deeply.'

Hill then quoted from the letter: 'You may think it silly and, as you say, a hopelessly inadequate reason for what I have done, but he [the puppy] was all I had and I loved that dog more than anything in the world, and there was nothing I would not do at the time to obtain revenge for his death.' Mike Merritt, with some justification, had interpreted this as motivation for O'Grady opting to spy for Germany in wartime.

Peter Hill hadn't reached the same conclusion, but in quoting another extract from one of Dorothy's 1940 letters to her lawyer, sent on 31 October, he seemed to be adding fuel to the case put forward by Merritt, who had referred to it himself as a key pointer to her treachery. Again, Hill provided some fascinating detail.

'I have no wish to help this country,' Dorothy had written. 'I hate it, or rather the authorities in it, too much to ever want to assist them. I have waited some 16 years for this.' For what? To spy for the enemy of Britain or simply to outwit and fool the country's wartime establishment for a laugh? That wasn't clear.

Interestingly, while she had gone to some lengths to defend herself against that initial prostitution conviction, in effect claiming that she hadn't been soliciting at all, O'Grady had said nothing about the three similar convictions that followed. If she really hadn't plied the streets of Soho for trade as a prostitute on that first occasion, it seemed abundantly clear that, later, she certainly had done so.

Whatever lay behind Dorothy's decision to go on the run in 1940 – and it was now even harder to tell – Peter Hill was certain of one thing: 'She was thrilled by the chase.' He had accepted her claim that, 'in a way she wanted to be caught, which is probably why she had sketches on her and in her room [at the Totland guest house] which were easily discovered' – and similarly the little swastika flag. 'Not the action of a professional spy!' he noted, echoing Dorothy's own words.

'When she cut the wires,' added Hill – apparently in no real doubt that she had done so, despite her protestations to the contrary:

... it was probably with a pair of nail scissors or small penknife found in her handbag; no wire-cutters or shears were found when her house was searched. And, when arrested for a second time, it was not the traditional spy's cyanide pill she rook, it was 20 tablets of ephedrine hydrochloride from a small bottle in her handbag – pills used sometimes to unblock a stuffy nose. Another gesture and totally ineffective.

So was the apparent suicide attempt while she was with the police in Yarmouth a sham? Not according to Dorothy. Peter Hill revealed that she had given her solicitor the impression that it may have been a genuine bid to escape the consequences of her re-arrest at Totland Bay. In a letter to him, she wrote, 'I was afraid those past charges would be brought up ... that was one of the reasons I carried those tablets on me and why I took them at Yarmouth ... as I would rather have been dead than have those things brought up after seventeen years.'

If she was speaking the truth on this matter – and it was, as always, virtually impossible to know whether or not she was – her professed dread at what might be revealed at her trial was at odds with her later claims to have enjoyed the court proceedings which did indeed reveal her past crimes en route to the death sentence.

The trial itself, wrote Peter Hill, was:

a travesty of justice. The facts about her actions, from a string of military, police and intelligence witnesses, were indisputable. The question was, had she acted against the national interest with intent to assist the enemy and damage the war effort, or just made a damn nuisance of herself to fulfil a silly woman's fantasy.

This was, of course, the crux of the whole Dorothy O'Grady story, the oft-repeated conundrum. 'Unfortunately,' added Hill, 'the police do not seem to have asked the question.'

And, as Hill had discovered when he interviewed her in 1962, O'Grady was not given the opportunity in court to answer it and tell the truth, as she insisted she would have done – though this remains very much a matter for conjecture to this day.

In fact, the trial transcript had shown that, not only had Dorothy remained silent at the trial, her counsel, John Scott Henderson, had offered no evidence on her behalf. He had relied solely on his summing-up to the jury, the essence of which was that Dorothy O'Grady was a silly woman, a *stupid* woman – but not a spy.

There was no proof, he insisted, that she had conspired with anyone else to aid the enemy, only that she had committed 'some unlawful acts which constituted misdemeanours'. Scott Henderson agreed that she admitted to MI5 that she had cut the communication wires, but had done so out of spite, 'so that the guns could not go into action'.

In a nutshell, she was a Nazi spy, an enemy saboteur, only in the narrow, peculiar confines of the fantasy world she had chosen to inhabit when that young Sandown police constable called to ask what she had been doing on the beach.

Did John Scott Henderson believe his closing address at Winchester would be sufficient for her to evade the death penalty? If what O'Grady said about his apparent lack of commitment to her cause is to be believed, the question might be, did he really care? Did she irritate him as much as it seems she had irritated the police, the military, the intelligence service and probably the Crown's legal establishment? We shall probably never know the answers to these questions. They are incidentals. The only one that mattered in December 1940 was – did the jury accept Scott Henderson's portrayal of Dorothy O'Grady as the spy who never was?

They did not.

Peter Hill, however, did. Rounding off his lengthy article for the *British Journalism Review*, he insisted that 'however much MI5 then wanted to believe it', O'Grady had certainly not committed her series of wartime crimes for the benefit of the Third Reich. 'I am convinced that she did it for herself to satisfy her need for revenge on the authorities and her craving for self-importance. Like the boy who cried "wolf", she told untruths so often that, when the truth might have emerged, no-one wanted to believe her.'

When the dust had settled on the 1995 disclosures and reflection illuminated the realities, it seemed abundantly clear that lies, contradictions and half-truths still littered and obstructed the undulating route to a proper understanding of Dorothy's story. There remained a long way to go. It would be another decade, into another century and a new millennium, before the O'Grady see-saw would finally settle.

## Notes

1   By the 1920s, Soho's noted night life, established after the First World War, was peopled by a floating population from all corners of the world, offering regular business for the prostitutes who plied its streets.

2   It is just possible that Dorothy O'Grady might instead have been referring to the army's radar installation at Culver Down Battery. As noted in Chapter 3, the CHL was operational at Culver for a brief experimental period only in July 1940 before being moved 1,500yd to the west, to a permanent location at Fort Bembridge. It was operating from there by 30 July so, if this was what O'Grady had noted on her map, she had been fortunate to spot it during its short period of activity at the Culver battery. A further, equally improbable, possibility is that her reference related to the mobile reserve equipment which stood in for RAF Ventnor's damaged radar facility, attacked twice by the Luftwaffe in August 1940. Far more likely is that Dorothy had correctly identified the Royal Navy's wireless station.

3   Rose Murphy did, of course, exist – but the celebrated American singer-pianist (of *Busy Line* fame), who died in 1989, can probably be eliminated from enquiries in the context of wartime espionage in the UK.

4   Ephedrine hydrochloride (HCl) has long been widely used as a stimulant. It is also employed as an appetite suppressant, concentration aid and decongestant, and is additionally used to treat hypotension associated with anaesthesia.

5   Major Sir Edward Tindal Atkinson (1878–1957) served as Director of Public Prosecutions between 1930 and 1944, playing a key role in framing the Defence Regulations under which Dorothy O'Grady was initially charged. Earlier in his career as a barrister, Atkinson had been awarded the CBE

and appointed Chevalier of the Legion d'honneur for his work at the peace conference following the First World War.

6  Sir Ernley Blackwell (1868–1944), called to the Bar in 1892, acted as chief justice for periods in 1933, 1937, 1938 and 1941, but is probably best remembered for his prominent role, while serving as legal adviser to the Cabinet, in the celebrated prosecution of Sir Roger Casement, executed for treason in 1916.

7  Sir Harry Hinsley (1918–98) was a highly regarded English historian and cryptanalyst, who worked at Bletchley Park (Station X) during the Second World War. He wrote extensively on the history of international relations and British intelligence during the war. Awarded the OBE in 1946, he was knighted in 1985.

8  The Southampton-based newspaper has since changed its title from *Southern Evening Echo* to *Southern Daily Echo*.

9  Hinsley edited the official history of British intelligence in the Second World War. A huge project, it eventually ran to several volumes, published between 1979 and 1990. An abridged edition of the work followed in 1993, published by Cambridge University Press.

10 SNOW was the British code name for Arthur Owens (1899–1957), a Welsh electrical engineer recruited by Germany as an intelligence agent in the Second World War before he was successfully 'turned' by MI5.

# 9

# INSIGHT FROM INSIDE: A VERY PECULIAR GIRL

The revised media-fuelled legacy of Dorothy O'Grady as the Second World War's oddest unmasked, double-bluffing traitor passed into the twenty-first century without further challenge. Yet the doubters continued to have doubts and the paradox remained: while O'Grady had undoubtedly been guilty of spying in 1940, this did not necessarily make her a spy – not in the accepted sense of the term.

Certainly, there was no proof that she had actually passed on to the enemy any of the detailed information she had gathered, or that she had ever intended to do so. The already persuasive suggestion that it had all been an elaborate attempt on O'Grady's part to attract attention to herself, a high-risk bid for fame – or infamy – was about to acquire powerful new support from an influential source. It came, retrospectively, in the form of an entry made in his diary on 17 December 1940, the day O'Grady's trial concluded at Winchester, by Guy Liddell, then the MI5 officer in charge of Britain's counter-espionage.

Published in 2005, among other excerpts from Liddell's wartime jottings, it read, 'Mrs O'Grady has been sentenced to death. Personally, I doubt whether she is guilty of anything more than collecting information. She probably pictured herself as a master spy, and cannot bring herself to say that there was really nothing behind it at all.' Apparently, this was Liddell's only reference to Dorothy.[1]

With the O'Grady case still open to interpretation – as was Dorothy herself – it had become clear that there was a need to get 'inside her head', posthumously, in a way that reached beyond the careful image of herself she had liked to portray.

The opportunity to do this, via the instincts and insight of the professionals who came into contact with O'Grady during her criminal career, and the records they compiled of her demeanour and behaviour while under lock and key, presented itself in the form of the Freedom of Information Act, which had entered the UK statute books in 2000. For there was another set of revealing papers, yet to be researched, on Dorothy O'Grady – her prison file. This extensive collection of documents had not been released into the public domain and it would be another decade or more before it was due for release as an open file.

Making the case that the information within the file was probably vital in establishing the truth about O'Grady's wartime activities, and that this was of significant relevance and importance to the country, the Isle of Wight in particular, I sought its release early in 2007 on grounds of public interest. The Home Office raised no objection. On 22 February O'Grady's prison file was made available for public viewing at The National Archives (the newly restyled title for the Public Record Office) in Kew. Or rather, a redacted version of the file. Some of the information it held, I was told, was covered by a Section Forty exemption to the Act as it contained 'personal information about a third party that is someone other than the enquirer'. Releasing it would contravene the terms of the Data Protection Act. However, even a 'weeded' version of the file held out the hope of clarifying the true character and motivation of the late Mrs O'Grady.

But the journey through the twists and turns to the truth about Dorothy has itself been obstructed by unexpected diversions which have made the task anything but straightforward. A wholly unexpected development threatened to impose a permanent road block on the quest just as the prison records had arrived on the scene. No sooner had access to these been granted, the breakthrough was seriously offset by disturbing news which threw a whole new set of questions into the equation and, for a while, questioned the validity of the project.

As arrangements were made with The National Archives (TNA) to view the newly released file for the first time, I asked simultaneously to review the documents released in 1995 which included the background to, and evidence from, the December 1940 trial, the material which had seemed to nail O'Grady as a bona fide spy. This should have been a straightforward request – *that* Home Office file (HO45/25408) had been in the public domain for more than twelve years, available for inspection at Kew. Not any longer, it appeared. In an email from TNA dated 8 March 2007, I was told the file in question had been 'lost by the Home Office'. The email continued, 'We sent it to them in February 2006 and requested its return in October, and were informed that they had lost it.'

There were two issues here. First, how did the Home Office manage to 'lose' a set of documents to which the public had been given access more than a decade earlier? Second, why, after so long a period in the public domain, had they asked to see the archived file in 2006? Was it merely to revise the contents, possibly by releasing further documents previously withheld? Or had the Home Office taken what seemed, on the face of it, an unlikely renewed interest in Dorothy O'Grady, sixty-seven years after she was caught apparently spying for Nazi Germany? There was to be no simple explanation on either point in the spring of 2007.

Instead, the Information and Record Management Service at the Home Office stoked the fire of intrigue by denying that they had lost the O'Grady documents and maintaining that '… this file was returned to The National Archives at Kew on 8 June 2006'. They had records to support this, they told me, adding, 'We are therefore content that from a Home Office perspective … this file is not lost and was successfully returned to Kew.' But Kew didn't have the file. What was going on?

Eventually, in mid-April 2007, I heard from The National Archives that the mystery of the missing file was now the subject of an internal investigation. This was in the hands of Geoff Baxter, Special

Productions Manager at Kew's Document Services Department, whose role included liaison with other government departments about archived material. He promised both an immediate start to his enquiries and periodic updates. The first update came on 27 April, two weeks into his mission. There was, said Mr Baxter, 'nothing of consequence to report'. He added that he would be 'exploring all the channels at my disposal' in his bid to find the elusive documents. Subsequent updates have mirrored the first.

Geoff Baxter has done his best. Yet nearly six years have elapsed and the file relating to Dorothy O'Grady's arrest, remand, trial and conviction has still not turned up; officially 'lost while on loan to government department'. Where has it gone? Both the Home Office and The National Archives now agree that it was returned to Kew in June 2006. Has it inadvertently – to put it kindly – been mislaid? This seems highly likely, but there are those who prefer to read something more complex into the file's disappearance, suggesting the Home Office have deliberately kept hold of it for some secret, perhaps sinister or possibly protective – maybe to safeguard the reputation of MI5 in wartime – purpose, ignoring the fact that its contents had been in the public domain for years.

These conspiracy theories can almost certainly be dismissed but the question remained – why did the Home Office request the return of the file in 2006? Having had no response to an informal enquiry along those lines, in September 2010 I formally sought the reason for the file's return in a further Freedom of Information Act application. When the reply was posted online, it revealed very little.

Confirming that the file had still not been located, a spokesman for the Home Office's Information Rights Team said the file's loan from TNA had been requested in February 2006 'for review purposes'. He added, 'It is likely that it was needed to help us decide on whether other files should be presented at TNA and, if so, whether they should be opened to the public from the time of transfer.' There was no indication from the Home Office as to the identity of the 'other files'. Was this a reference to the prison documents released in 2007 or is the government in possession of further O'Grady records? It remains a mystery.

The Home Office view is that these archives have been 'swallowed' by another, unrelated, file. 'Our experience shows that files can sometimes be placed accidentally inside another file,' they explained. 'When this happens it is only the outside file cover that has its movements recorded and any misplaced file can be sitting within one of several files that get transferred on a daily basis.' It's a view now shared by TNA. File HO45/25408 lies hidden inside another file of archived documents among the millions at Kew, awaiting the day it is found by chance when – if? – that concealing file is requested for research purposes.

There was some brighter news – though it amounted to scant consolation in the context of the O'Grady case – as the Home Office response continued, 'Our procedures for the recall and return of TNA files have been reviewed to reduce the risk of such a situation arising in future ...' Meanwhile, their spokesman added, the search for file HO45/25408 would continue. 'Should this misplaced file come to light ... then we will notify you and assess whether it can be released.'

The file's contents were known. They had been examined. Their disappearance, however, ruled out the opportunity to cross-check new evidence as it came to light. Also lost was access to the file's photographic archive, the evidential pictures used at O'Grady's trial. There had seemed no urgency in obtaining copies. Those photographs, that file of papers, had seemed absolutely secure in the care of the nation's archival custodians. Was the project to establish the truth about Dorothy O'Grady now fatally flawed? The answer, after due consideration, was – no, it wasn't. The separately filed prison records saved the day.

In parallel with a detailed inspection of these 'new' documents, a thorough search was made of all available references to Dorothy's familial background and formative years in an attempt to track the path that led her to prison in the first place – filling in the gaps between the piecemeal information already to hand.

The earliest accessible pointer to Dorothy O'Grady appears in the census return for 1901. Aged 3, she is shown as living with her adoptive parents, George and Pamela Squire, at 54 Lynette Avenue on the south side of Clapham, close to Clapham Common's historic expanse of grassland. Dorothy's adoption as a newly born infant, which apparently followed an initial period of foster care, had filled a major void in the lives of the otherwise childless couple. Who her birth parents were remains a mystery. Adoption (and fostering) of children had taken place informally for centuries in Britain, by private arrangement, but it was not until the 1920s that the practice became legally recognised and recorded, more than two decades after Dorothy's adoption by the Squires in 1897.

George Squire, aged 50 at the time the census was taken, is described as a library attendant at the British Museum, born in the village of Stow, near Sleaford, Lincolnshire. The birthplace of his 47-year-old wife is given as 'Cranley, Whittering'. Though the addition of 'Whittering' is confusing – suggesting a possible misspelling of Wittering, near Peterborough, or the Witterings in West Sussex – this is more likely to have been a reference to Cranleigh village in Surrey. The spelling had been changed from Cranley in the nineteenth century to avoid postal confusion with Crawley, but the former spelling would still have been in use when Pamela was born in 1854. The spelling of Squire without a final 's' is at odds with several of Dorothy's later criminal records, which refer to her family name as Squires – presumably a clerical error.

The 1901 census data also reveals that Dorothy had a playmate at the Lynette Avenue house, her older cousin Phyllis Scrivener, the daughter of Pamela's 36-year-old sister, Harriet Scrivener, the fifth member of the Clapham household. Born in Northampton, Phyllis was six weeks short of her fifth birthday when the census was taken on the night of 31 March 1901. There is no reference to her father.

Dorothy's apparently short-lived convent education as a young girl is hard to determine, but it seems likely that her adoptive parents took advantage of the proximity at Clapham Common of the Convent of Notre Dame, which since 1861 had been run as a school by an order of Roman Catholic nuns from Belgium.[2, 3]

Everything had changed by the time of the next census in 1911. As revealed in the earlier disclosures from the records released in 1995, Pamela Squire had died in 1908, three years before the census, leaving Dorothy motherless at just 10 years old. George, now promoted to Chief Attendant at the British Museum's repository, had engaged a housekeeper and, early in 1910, aged 60, he had married her. Dorothy's grief at her adoptive mother's death, compounded by the hasty installation of 41-year-old Marian Bird as her father's second wife, certainly seems to have had the profound effect on her formative years that she had much later described. The resentment she expressed at Marian Bird's supplanting of her beloved mother appears to have been genuine. Did Dorothy rebel? The census of 1911 suggests that this was very probably the case. When it was taken in mid-April, the 13-year-old girl had left the family home – and Clapham.

Instead, she was living in central London, at what the census enumerator described as the St John's Hostel Training School in Great Western Road, Paddington. More commonly recalled as St John's Training School for Girls, this establishment, which had been in operation under various guises for nearly half a century, provided hostel accommodation for girls who were being trained there for domestic service. On the night the census was taken, there were twenty-four girls in residence, their ages ranging from 9 to 15. Their 'position in institution' was somewhat pitifully listed on the return as 'inmate'.[4,5]

No documentary evidence remains as to whether Dorothy ever returned to her home. The likelihood is that she went straight from the training school into service – possibly her employment as a 17-year-old with the Rector of Christ Church in Harrow was her first as a servant. Her subsequent career in domestic drudgery is unclear. Very probably unhappy, unfulfilled and still resentful, it would not be many years before Dorothy Squire had succumbed to the lure of crime.

The prison records opened for public inspection in 2007 showed that Dorothy had been something of an enigma from the first time she fell foul of the law as a young woman in the closing period of the First

World War. Not unattractive in her two-profile 'mug shot' photographs, but already bespectacled beneath a wide-brimmed hat, the 20-year-old Dorothy – arrested and charged under the name of Pamela Arland, her first recorded use of the alias – was the subject of a 'reception report' compiled by the governor of Holloway prison on 31 January 1918 following her initial criminal conviction on the charge of forging banknotes. This partially disintegrated document provides the earliest professional insight into the background and character of the future Dorothy O'Grady.

Confirming her date and place of birth as 25 October 1897 at Clapham Common and her status as a single woman, it lists her professed religion as Church of England – suggesting her brief convent education had turned her against Roman Catholicism – and her most recent place of residence as lodgings at 36 Star Street in the north London suburb of Edgware. Details of her parents or next of kin, and her relationship with them, are conspicuous by their absence. With both her adoptive parents no longer alive, Dorothy presumably had seen no reason for mentioning the existence of her surviving stepmother, Marian. In fact, it seems she gave no familial details at all to the governor, who had simply written 'Unknown'. The 1918 prison document describes 'Miss Arland' as a servant whose employer immediately prior to her arrest had been a Mrs Chambers at 6 Walton Place, Chelsea, in the south-west of London.

Intriguingly, the governor did not record on the document Dorothy's previous place of employment before the Chelsea engagement, nor her reasons for leaving. Instead, the prison chief had inserted a name, 'Mr Thompson', describing him as secretary of the 'London Preventative Institution' at 200 Euston Road. This was 'shorthand' for W.W. Thompson and a charitable organisation set up in 1857 with the highly descriptive and somewhat grandiose full title of London Female Preventative & Reformatory Institution (Friendless and Fallen). Evidently, the young and clearly troubled 'Miss Arland' had spent time at the Euston Road facility before that first court appearance in January 1918.

So, what did the governor make of prisoner 7250 in this initial assessment of a woman destined to be the subject of many more in the years that were to follow? Revealingly, he wrote that she was 'intelligent and bright', adding, 'Her past history shows that she is disturbed and not industrious or of good character. Her associates are probably bad. She has strong criminal tendencies and needs to be detained for her own reformation.' It was for this reason, the governor noted, that she had been recommended for a period of Borstal detention.

The sentence of three years' Borstal training had been handed down at the Old Bailey the previous day. The prison papers disclosed for the first time the far from straightforward nature of this initial period of incarceration – a troublesome portend of things to come. It was, in fact, not until 23 April that Dorothy Squire, under her assumed name of Pamela Arland, was transferred from Holloway to the Borstal at Aylesbury in Buckinghamshire. She stayed there for only nineteen months. In a report compiled some time later by the Borstal Association, reference was made to her behaviour at Aylesbury. 'She was said to be incorrigible,' it read, 'and in November 1919 her Borstal sentence was commuted to imprisonment. She was removed to HM Prison Maidstone.' This, apparently, was quickly deemed inappropriate and on 1 December, less than two years after her sentencing at the Old Bailey, she was discharged from prison.

Exasperated, the authorities had sent her instead back to the care of W.W. Thompson at Parsons Green, Fulham, the location of one of the London Female Preventative & Reformatory Institution's several residential homes. Matters then went from bad to worse. Within two months, on 20 January 1920, the Institution's secretary had himself become exasperated by her uncooperative attitude.

'I am very sorry to say,' he wrote to the governor at Maidstone prison, who retained ultimate responsibility for the hard to control young woman, 'that, after several reports made to me as to this girl's behaviour, our Superintendent yesterday felt she could not keep the girl in the Home any longer ...' Pamela Arland, he added, had consequently been transferred temporarily to the tighter security of the institution's probationary home in Liverpool Street, Kings Cross. 'I think the girl is safer there than at Parsons Green,' added Thompson, 'as it would be far more difficult to abscond should she try to do this.' He explained that:

> Pamela has objected to do work given her to do and has been exceedingly insolent and insubordinate in front of the other inmates over and over again and, at last, the Superintendent felt it was absolutely necessary in the interests of the other inmates that Pamela should no longer be kept in the Home.

Despairingly, Thompson, who copied his letter to the prison commissioners, asked for advice as to which course of action, given the trying circumstances, he should now adopt. He then added a passage to his letter which, in the light of subsequent events, today has particular relevance:

> I am exceedingly disappointed and did hope that the girl would strive to do well. I have seen her this morning and she stated she would rather be in Prison than stay in the Home, as she was told in Prison she was such a good girl, and was so much praised up that she thought that was the best place for her to be. She also stated that the Chaplain there knew all about her and asked her, when she was free, to make him a 10s/- Treasury Note like those in respect of which she was charged. In fact, she picks up little things that are said and magnifies them for her own benefit, and makes out that everybody is ill-using her in her present surroundings.

In sending to the prison commissioners in London the copy of his letter, Thompson enclosed a covering note. It amounted to a further plea for help in dealing with a girl 'who has a very peculiar disposition'. For some years, he told the commissioners:

> I have been very anxious ... to try and do my utmost to prevent her going down, or further down. Unfortunately, she has, by her own recent behaviour,

prevented my keeping her in the Home and I am a little surprised to find that she is practically free, and I fear the result in her case may be that at any future time she will think she has only got to play up and misbehave herself to bring about what she desires ... Can you inform me whether you have any hold at all upon her as, if not, I must do the best I can under the circumstances so that she may not think she has derived any great advantage from her misbehaviour ...

Thompson signed off his despairing note by offering to meet with the commissioners, 'if you could kindly grant me an interview'.

There was little doubt which part of his letter would most concern the prison commissioners. The suggestion that the prison chaplain at Maidstone had asked the troublesome young offender to make him a 10$s$ banknote must surely have seemed the stuff of wild fantasy on her part to the recipients of Thompson's correspondence but, naturally, such a serious allegation had to be investigated. The governor at Maidstone was asked by the prison commissioners to request from the chaplain 'his observations'. Unsurprisingly, the chaplain strongly denied the accusation and was fully exonerated. The future Dorothy O'Grady, it seems, had already shown herself to be a mistress of fantasy.

By the end of January 1920, Thompson had been told by the prison commissioners, probably to his dismay, that they had 'no further hold' on her. He was left to try and convince his reluctant, rebellious charge of the error of her ways.

It was evidently a task too far for this dedicated official and his institution colleagues. Free from any kind of formal jurisdiction, 'Pamela Arland' soon left London. By mid-June 1920 the 'peculiar' girl had been remanded at Brighton's borough police court until the 14th of that month on a charge of larceny – stealing clothes as a servant. She had committed the offence while in service in the Sussex seaside town. The sentence of two years' hard labour had seemed severe when it first come to light among the wartime trial records released in 1995. The prison papers provided a context – Dorothy's earlier failure to respond to the help offered in London – which made it easier to understand.

Not that it worked. Within a year of completing this, she was yet again in trouble.

Back in London, she was arrested in the spring of 1923 for loitering as a prostitute among the night life of the city's colourfully cosmopolitan Soho district – the charge which would later feature so prominently in her story. The newly released prison file provided more detail to augment that already known. On 29 May, prosecuted under her real name of Dorothy Squire (though the documentation added the erroneous final 's'), she appeared before the police court at Marlborough Street where she was fined 30*s* (£1.50 – roughly equivalent at the time to the average labourer's wages for three ten-hour days' work).

She was back before the Marlborough Street court on 10 March 1925, again charged as Dorothy Squires, for soliciting as a prostitute – another 30*s* fine – and reappeared at the same court for a similar offence on 16 June the same year. This time the fine was increased to 40*s* (£2) with the option of a month in prison. The indications are that she opted to serve the jail sentence.

O'Grady's final police court appearance in the 1920s, this time at Bow Street, followed on 31 July 1926 and resulted in her fourth conviction for prostitution. As noted in Chapter 8, the penalty for this was another £2 fine or twenty-one days' imprisonment, the termination of which would have exactly coincided with her wedding day on 21 August. Whether she paid up or was sent down, it is hard to believe that she could have kept secret from her groom knowledge of her recent crimes.

She would claim to have done exactly that, of course, and the letters she sent from her remand cell at Holloway in 1940 certainly seem to support this. It is possible only to conclude that she spun Vincent O'Grady another great 'yarn' to cover her criminal tracks. Either that or Vincent was fully aware of his bride's career on the streets of London prior to the wedding. There is no proof that this was how they met but, given the circumstances, it must at least be regarded as possible.

Did Vincent find respectable accommodation for her in eastern Essex, well away from Dorothy's dubious London connections and the unwholesome environment of Soho? This, too, seems likely, though at precisely what stage she took up residence at 39 Cherry Gardens Road, Maldon, remains a mystery. Universal suffrage for women was not achieved until 1928 and Dorothy did not qualify for the vote under the restrictions in force prior to this. The town's electoral registers for the period, therefore, would not have included her on the roll.

Listed at the Cherry Gardens Road address on the registers published in 1926 was the grandly named Albion James Mead. The 55-year-old man, a butcher by trade, was a member of a well-known Essex family who seems to have owned more than one property in Maldon at the time of the O'Grady wedding. He and his wife, Ethel – more commonly known by her second name, Maria – were, confusingly, also registered in 1926 at an address in the Essex town's Spital Road. An inspection of the electoral rolls for the years that followed suggests that 39 Cherry Gardens Road may have offered lodging accommodation for single women. Whatever the truth of that, there is one other certainty about Dorothy's link to the Meads in Maldon – Maria Mead acted as a witness at the register office wedding on 21 August, along with John Trollope, a friend of Vincent's.

Essex had served its purpose. Once married, the O'Gradys seem to have returned to London and the environs of Vincent's work as a firefighter in the East End. That he was a steadying influence on Dorothy there can be little doubt. She finally settled down. It can be no coincidence that it was not until the couple were separated thirteen years later by the outbreak of war that she was again in trouble.

The pre-war prison records of Dorothy O'Grady's criminal career had filled in the gaps, provided clarification and offered a series of revealing new glimpses of her troubled background and character as a young woman. Yet it was those relating to her arrest in 1940 and subsequent imprisonment that painted the most comprehensive picture of her enigmatic personality and amount to the most compelling of pointers in the quest to establish her status as a traitor or tease.

That she was a very odd candidate for an indulgence in espionage was strikingly obvious from the earliest of the wartime documents filed among her newly released prison papers – a letter to the Isle of Wight constabulary's superintendent from Detective Inspector Harry Rogers of Ryde CID, dated 17 October 1940, the day after O'Grady was sent for trial by the town's magistrates. DI Rogers described how Dorothy had been transferred from Holloway jail on 14 October into his custody at Ryde police station, where she was to remain for two nights before and during her committal to Winchester Assizes.

'During the whole of the time, she was attended by my wife and had many conversations with her,' Rogers told his superintendent in Newport. What O'Grady said to Mrs Rogers, and the inspector duly noted in his letter, throws considerable light on some of the intriguing references, filed among the earlier released trial records, to Dorothy's bizarre behaviour while on remand at Holloway.

'Soon after her arrival here,' wrote DI Rogers, 'she informed my wife that she had had a day's solitary confinement at Holloway prison on bread and water. She said that the reason for this was that her cell was on about the third floor of the prison and one night, during an air raid, a light was reported to be seen emanating from a window on this floor.' The message from the prison gate, O'Grady had confided to Mrs Rogers, was that the light was flashing and prison staff had quickly concluded that it could only have come from Dorothy's cell.

'She did not contradict this and was immediately removed to another cell on the ground floor,' added the inspector's report of his short-term prisoner's apparently candid, highly detailed and unsolicited account. 'The cell she had previously occupied was examined and an electric bulb was found in her bed. She had obtained the bulb from another inmate of the prison. She received punishment for this but did not mind being punished for what she knew was wrong.'

Whatever previous experience DI Rogers (a future Mayor of Ryde) had of suspected enemy agents, it must surely have struck him as unusual, to put it mildly, that O'Grady had been so keen to discuss with the detective's wife what seemed a blatant act of treachery on her part. Rogers' report suggests that his temporary charge was revelling in her status as a suspected spy – and just couldn't stop blabbing about it.

Towards the end of her lengthy chats with Mrs Rogers, O'Grady had – proudly, it seems – told the officer's wife that she had been found wearing a swastika badge at the Ryde hearing. 'She said she had made a number of them at Holloway prison and had given some to the other inmates there,' noted DI Rogers.

Dorothy's association with a Russian woman suspected of working for the Germans (to which reference had also been made in the trial records made public in 1995) was the subject of another illuminating passage in the inspector's letter. He recounted Dorothy's comments to his wife about 'a Russian lady' O'Grady had met while on remand at the jail, a woman, she had asserted, working for the enemy 'in the Secret Service Agency'. Rogers' account continued, 'They conversed together and she [O'Grady] asked her advice as to what she should tell her solicitor. The Russian lady said she should just outline the case to him but, as they were under a vow of secrecy, they could not divulge anything of a secret nature.' Evidently, O'Grady had not revealed, or Mrs Rogers had failed to note, the identity of this apparent fellow Nazi agent in the jail.

DI Rogers' fullsome report made clear that, for a woman under a supposed vow of secrecy, Dorothy O'Grady had been remarkably loose-tongued in providing the inspector's wife with a very chatty account of her 'many conversations with the other inmates about the German invasions which would take place'. According to O'Grady's reported remarks, the outcome of these discussions, which usually took place during visits to the lavatories, was that her fellow prisoners 'were now beginning to think her way and would go out and spread it about'. O'Grady had told Mrs Rogers that the Germans 'knew every field in the country; they also knew when they were ploughed up and just what was taking place'.

The talkative prisoner had also volunteered information on the plans and sketches of military defences she freely admitted she had drawn, information that would certainly have been of potential use to the enemy if she had passed it on. DI Rogers added, 'She said that those the police had now were only duplicates of what she had sent away in August last.' However, as befitted a professed secret agent, she had 'definitely refused to give any information to anyone as to this. It was so involved and began low and gradually grew up. She had received no money … and what she was doing was for spite, to get her revenge for something that happened years ago when she was wrongfully fined'.

This, it would seem, was Dorothy O'Grady's first hint at the motivation which lay behind her apparent spying activity – the bitter grudge she bore against the British authorities for that initial conviction in the 1920s for soliciting in London.

Inspector Rogers concluded his letter with a recommendation that a copy be sent to Lt. Colonel Edward Hinchley Cooke at MI5 'for information'. It may have helped the latter conclude that O'Grady's intelligence gathering was of 'vital importance' (see Chapter 8). Yet, if he also read – as surely he would have done – a subsequent report compiled by the governor at Holloway on the issues raised by O'Grady in her series of chatty conversations at Ryde with Mrs Rogers, he must have had serious doubts about her credentials as an enemy agent.

The governor's report, prepared primarily for the prison commissioners, was written on 11 November. Initially referring back to events at the prison on 8 October, a week before the committal hearing at Ryde, it recalled a message relayed to the governor that O'Grady had been 'boasting to another prisoner on remand that she had the means to flash signals to the Germans'. A search had been made 'and there was found in her cell an electric light bulb which was one of the prison's stock, and a piece of rope similar to the sash cord used in the prison'.

Of this extraordinary episode, the governor's report merely added:

She was placed on report for being in unauthorised possession of prison property and after investigating … I punished her by ordering one day's close confinement and one day's restricted diet No. 1 … I was satisfied that she could not signal by means of this spare bulb … but on the grounds of security, I located her on the ground floor … The lights are switched off at the main during an alert period at night.[6]

139

Questioned, O'Grady had 'sought to explain the possession of the extra bulb by saying that an officer had taken away the bulb in her cell the night before. This was not true. She would not state where she got the rope, nor what she intended to do with it.'

O'Grady's claim that a flashing light had been reported by staff at the prison gate was dismissed outright by the governor. There had been no such message. 'A prisoner in another wing did report that she saw a light flashing but this was not traced to O'Grady. We get frequent reports of 'lights flashing' which on investigation are found to have a simple explanation,' the governor's account explained.

It seems that the only signal Dorothy had succeeded in flashing from her prison cell was to alert her Holloway jailers to the state of her apparently disturbed mind.

The prison commissioners were told that the governor had not been overly concerned about the swastika O'Grady had worn in the Ryde courtroom, although it *was* one of many. 'I took no action concerning the swastika emblems she had embroidered,' the governor wrote. 'They were made with and on her own material. With certain of the internees at present detained under Regulation 18B, it has been a fashion at times to make or embroider on their clothing swastikas. I have dealt with this fashion by ignoring it – I think with success.'

While O'Grady, facing specific charges of espionage, was not herself detained under the provisions of Defence Regulation 18B, which allowed the internment of suspected Nazi sympathisers, she was evidently mixing at Holloway with women who *were* 18B detainees – and adopting their 'fashionable' activity. But what of that apparent association at the prison with 'the Russian lady' Inspector Rogers had mentioned in his earlier report from Ryde? The governor's report once again held the answer: 'I am of [the] opinion that the Russian lady referred to is Anna Wolkoff, but she [O'Grady] had no opportunity of carrying on any form of long conversation with this prisoner when they were both on remand.'[7]

At the time of the events described in the governor's report, Anna Wolkoff, a naturalised British citizen from a White Russian family, was awaiting trial at the Old Bailey for her leading role in the spy ring operated by members of the Right Club, a secret society – until it was infiltrated by MI5 – set up in May 1939 with the objective of unifying extreme right-wing political activity in Britain.

Wolkoff (whose fellow Right Club members included its founder, Archibald Ramsay, the Dukes of Wellington and Westminster, and the notorious propaganda broadcaster William Joyce – Lord Haw-Haw) was a key figure in Britain's pro-Nazi movement at the onset of war. She went on to serve seven years of a ten-year prison sentence following her conviction on 7 November 1940 for violating the Official Secrets Act. It would have been fascinating to have heard the verdict of this high-profile and undisputed Nazi sympathiser on Dorothy O'Grady, with whom she undoubtedly shared star billing for a short period at Holloway in 1940, but the opportunity for Wolkoff to provide such an insight was ended with her death in a car crash in Spain in 1973 at the age of 71.[8]

Whatever the nature of O'Grady's discussions with Anna Wolkoff in Holloway prison – if they took place at all – the governor was not unduly perturbed. 'I have no evidence that she [O'Grady] had propaganda talk with other women prisoners. Had she held such conversation, some prisoner would most certainly have reported the matter to us,' the prison commissioners were confidently assured.

The November 1940 report from Holloway's prison chief concluded with a pertinent comment on Dorothy's character as a remand prisoner awaiting her trial. 'O'Grady gave me the impression of being an unreliable informant who likes to attract attention by extravagant talk,' wrote the governor, mirroring broadly the assessments made two decades earlier of the young Dorothy as an attention-seeking fantasist – and neatly summarising the general perception of her prior to the release in 1995 of those apparently damning prosecution trial records.

It can be safely assumed that Holloway's governor and staff were relieved to see the back of the Isle of Wight landlady when, following the appeal in February 1941 that saved her life, she was moved to the Buckinghamshire jail at Aylesbury to begin the fourteen-year sentence imposed for the non-capital offences. From the documentary evidence now available, it is clear that O'Grady's change of secure accommodation did not produce a change in her behaviour.

# Notes

1 West, Nigel (ed.), *The Guy Liddell Diaries 1939–42* (Routledge, 2005).
2 No other evidence has been found to verify Dorothy's early involvement with Roman Catholicism.
3 The convent was founded by the Sisters of Notre Dame de Namur, an order originating in Amiens in 1803.
4 St John's Hostel (later St John's House), which adjoined Westbourne School, operated as a servants' training establishment until the 1930s, when the premises were converted into a social club.
5 Dorothy's birthplace on the census return was given as Clapham Common. This was her adoptive parents' area of residence. Surviving records do not indicate whether it was also that of her birth parents.
6 Restricted diet number one – bread and water.
7 Regulation 18B, the most controversial of the Defence Regulations, was widely used by Britain in the early period of the war. In 1940, at the height of the invasion scare, around 1,000 people were detained under its provisions. The number declined significantly as the war progressed until 18B was abolished in 1945.
8 Anna Wolkoff was tried in November 1940 at the Old Bailey with Tyler Kent (1911–88), a like-minded American diplomat who stole secret documents for pro-German contacts while working as a cypher clerk at the US Embassy in London. Wolkoff had introduced Kent to the Right Club and was implicated in his espionage as their relationship blossomed. Sentenced to seven years in jail, Kent was deported at the end of the war back to the USA. Despite his oft-proclaimed anti-communist views, he was for a long time suspected of being a secret Soviet sympathiser. He died in poverty in a Texas trailer park.

# 10

# SUBPLOT:
# VERA THE BEAUTIFUL SPY

Dorothy O'Grady's second term of penal detention at Aylesbury, where a little over two decades earlier she had so spectacularly failed to respond to Borstal training, is a story in itself, laced with drama, intrigue, poignancy, farce and disturbingly vivid revelation. It is tempting to move straight to the main plot, to unravel and then to unveil what I believe must surely stand as the final truth about this extraordinary, perplexing woman. Yet, Aylesbury prison may also hold a fascinating, if speculative, sub-plot in Dorothy's story – and in that of another headline-grabbing female in the history of Second World War espionage. This is as good a point as any to ask the question: was there a link between Dorothy O'Grady and the mysterious enemy agent they called 'the beautiful spy'?

There is an air of glamour to the story of Vera Schalburg that is singularly missing from the O'Grady saga. Forever young, Vera is not just beautiful in the only photographs which survive of her – she oozes the sexuality that seems to have been a notable feature of her life up to the 1940s and transcends the tiredness and anxiety all too obvious in those images, taken just a day after she was captured in Scotland on an ill-fated spying mission. It's an allure that has contributed greatly to the desire of many people, in several countries, to delve into the enduring mystery that surrounds her to this day. The release in recent years of previously secret documents has helped their cause to a significant degree. Yet, while this has brought clarity to some of the key facts, at the same time it has added murky new layers of mystery to the tale. It is hard to pluck the proverbial wood from the trees within the often conflicting accounts her present internet devotees have presented as facts. Their interpretations continue to vary.

From October 1940 onwards Vera's tale is hard to follow, with just the odd glimmer of patchy illumination to guide the seeker after facts. And it is still the case that nobody today can be sure of the story's ending. What happened to Vera after the war? Some biographers accept the apparently official British explanation that she was repatriated to Germany (though she was not actually a German national). Yet there is no shortage of those who prefer the romantic alternative that she remained in the UK and could conceivably still be in Britain today, although it would now have to be as a centenarian. As noted in Chapter 1, of the locations suggested for her post-war British residency, it is Dorothy O'Grady's old stamping ground, the Isle of Wight, that is most favoured.

There is some foundation for adhering to this as a possibility. If it is, or was, the truth, can the parallel post-war presence in the offshore isle of these two puzzling 'women of espionage' be put down to unlikely – some might say, astonishing – coincidence? Or are their respective stories in some other way intertwined? The prison at Aylesbury may hold the key. But in order to unlock the possibility of a link it is necessary to examine first the path which put Vera Schalburg on a roundabout route to spy for Nazi Germany, collide head-on with MI5 and then effectively disappear, to re-emerge only in cloak and dagger intrigue, mystique and speculation, but never again in recognisable flesh and blood.

So contradictory are the various accounts of Vera's story – a situation she appears to have fostered herself in misleading wartime interviews with British intelligence officers – that any attempt to chronicle her life plunges immediately into confusion. Most biographers opt for

December 1912 as the approximate date of her birth. This is what she told MI5 in 1940. Other researchers have come up with a wide range of alternatives – from 1909 to 1914.

Options are also given for *where* she was born and to whom. While records suggest that she was a native of Siberia and was the daughter of a Danish ex-patriot industrialist father and a Russian mother, there are those who cling to the theory that her birthplace was actually the Ukrainian city of Kiev and that her mother's origins lay in Polish-Ukrainian aristocracy. Another body of opinion, based on Vera's own wartime testament, suggests that she was, in fact, adopted as a small child, was very probably illegitimate and may have had Jewish parentage. All these versions of her background may hold elements of the truth, though it remains very much open to question. Spies lie. It's part of the job.

Whatever the realities of her background, the evidence suggests that Vera was not an only child. She seems to have had at least one brother, very possibly two. The probable identity of her older brother has been revealed – reliably it would appear – as Christian von Schalburg, a future Danish Nazi zealot. Many sources maintain that he played a significant role in Vera's pre-war life, a man whose widow has provided one of the clearest indicators to her post-war residency.[1]

If one of the most popular accounts of Vera's early life is accepted, the Schalburgs fled Siberia soon after the 1917 Bolshevik Revolution in imperial Russia to settle in Denmark, where they bought a farm on the Jutland peninsular. By 1924, while her older brother remained in Copenhagen as a soldier attached to Denmark's Royal Life Guards, Vera had moved with the rest of the family to Paris. As a teenager she attended ballet school in the city, becoming a professional ballerina. The story goes that she toured England in 1927 with the Trefilova ballet company and later appeared with the Ballets Russes in the Champs Elysees. However, by 1930, although still working in ballet, it appears she may simultaneously have been pursuing a second career through the probably more lucrative form of dancing offered amid the glamour of Parisian cabaret. It is said she embraced the cabaret circuit and made it to the Folies Bergeres. Male interest would certainly have followed and, if the next chapter of her story is correct – it is ignored totally by some researchers – one man who picked her out for special attention was to have a profound effect on her life.[2]

Count Sergei Ignatieff, runs the story, came from a once-prominent Russian aristocratic dynasty and, like Vera and her own family, he had left the motherland in the wake of the 1917 revolution. By now exiled in France, he had developed a noteworthy career as a professional spy. The adjectival term usually applied to Ignatieff is 'unscrupulous'. That, it would seem, is putting it mildly. MI5 had him marked down as 'a cocaine addict, a pervert and actively engaged in espionage for the White Russians'. It seems, however, that he was, in fact, a double agent, spying not only for Russia's anti-communist 'White' opposition but – on the face of it, at least – also for the Soviet communist regime's intelligence gathering service in Moscow. The conclusion can probably be drawn that he served only the one real master – himself. Count Ignatieff's complicated spying work, it is suggested, was complemented by his parallel and arguably more straightforward role as an international drug trafficker.[3]

Those who accept this version of events maintain that Sergei Ignatieff had a mesmerising effect on the young and impressionable Vera Schalburg. Vera suggested as much herself in 1940, adding that, under his spell, she became his mistress. There is further Vera-inspired evidence that they lived together as man and wife for a period – and may actually have married. There is also a suggestion that he used her as his drugs courier and that, in the course of carrying packages of Ignatieff's illicit substances across Europe over a period of up to seven years, Vera very possibly developed an addiction to cocaine herself.[4]

According to Vera, she was also being used by him as a spy in France. But on whose behalf? Bearing in mind her background, it would seem more likely that she was spying on the Soviet communists rather than for them. Unsurprisingly, there are a number of adherents to the contrary view among her biographers. The possibility that she, too, worked as a double agent at Ignatieff's behest would seem to suggest itself. The story continues that, in the mid-1930s, while the couple were living for a period in Brussels, Vera tried to break free from the vice-like grip and unrelenting control Ignatieff exercised over her. He responded to this by stabbing her in an apparent murder attempt. Yet, according to Vera, it was his later disappearance in Russia, where he was arrested and then executed as a spy by the Soviets, which finally allowed her to escape his clutches. Then, claimed Vera, out of necessity and fear, she transferred her allegiance as a proven spy to Nazi Germany's military intelligence service, the Abwehr.

The precise details of how and why Vera joined the Abwehr – she is believed to have been recruited in 1937 – are muddled, in typical Vera-lore fashion, by the conflicting interpretations of her career and personal life, and especially her complex marital and sexual history from the mid-1930s onwards. There have been suggestions that her recruitment can simply be put down to an understandable desire by the German agency to make use of her Russian contacts for an anti-communist espionage role. Like most aspects of Vera's story, it was probably not as straightforward as that. Her own version of how it came about smacks of melodrama. It might have happened – but it's hard to believe.

In essence, Vera related to MI5 how she had contacted the Abwehr after learning her name was on a Nazi 'black list' because the Germans knew of her spying missions for the Soviet Union – whether these were genuine or not. The information, she said, had come from an official of the Belgian counter-intelligence service in Brussels. That Vera could have had links with Belgium's secret services is believable. Whether or not she lived in Brussels for a while with the mysterious Ignatieff, it seems to be a fact that she and her family had moved to the city in 1933 and, if while there she had been involved in spying activity, Belgian intelligence would probably have known of this. Plausibility, however, is stretched by the 'black list' revelation. 'This is highly doubtful since it is difficult to imagine how a Belgian official could have got wind of a vague German "black list" ...' conclude Dutch researchers F.A.C. Kluiters and E. Verhoeyen in one of the more measured online accounts of Vera's life story.[5]

Fearful of potential German 'retaliation', Vera explained, she had sought advice from her soldier brother, Christian, who was by then heavily involved in far right politics in Denmark as an active member of the country's own Nazi movement. It was he who arranged her introduction to the Abwehr in Germany. Eventually, via a string of Abwehr contacts, Vera was shaking hands with Major Hilmar Dierks, a vastly experienced intelligence officer attached to the agency's Hamburg branch. Dierks, who was 48 in 1937, twenty years older than Vera, took to her in every sense. She was soon one of his agents – and his mistress.[6]

Vera's earliest work for the Abwehr appears to have involved spying on Soviet intelligence sources in Belgium. Despite claims that she quickly became one of Germany's outstanding female secret agents, there is little evidence to support the view that these initial assignments were in any real sense productive. Neither does the suggestion that she and Dierks were married at a Hamburg register office in October 1937 have any unquestionable basis in fact, though it remains a possibility. Vera muddied these marital waters during her MI5 interrogation three years later by claiming she had actually married somebody else – Sturig by name. Her interrogator, unable to tease any corroborative evidence from her, treated this claim with scepticism. Kluiters and Verhoeyen suggest it was a good example of Vera's several attempts at creating a smokescreen to obscure the truth. The balance of probability suggest they are right.

Many accounts of Vera's life maintain that in the year preceding the outbreak of war with Britain in September 1939 she was sent by the Abwehr to London. Again, there are contradictory interpretations. One version suggests that this was in 1938 and that Vera was accompanied by Dierks. Others place her visit in 1939 – claiming that it ended when she left in a hurry in the days following the war's outbreak – and do not refer to Dierks at all. Whether or not he travelled with her, the general plan was apparently for Vera to mix socially with fellow German agents in the UK, Nazi sympathisers and other influential people who might reveal snippets of information of potential use to the Abwehr.

Kluiters and Verhoeyen, who opt for a 1939 setting, suggest that she had been loaned by Dierks to his colleague Nikolaus Ritter, who was prominently engaged in the Abwehr's intelligence-gathering work for the Luftwaffe. Vera, say the Dutch researchers, was to stay with one of Ritter's contacts in London, the Duchess de Château-Thierry, who counted prominent RAF officers within her wide social circle.

The idea was for the Duchess to open a tearoom, to which the officers would be invited and where Vera would mix with the clientele, gain their confidence and try to worm what information she could out of them about RAF strength and the officers' feelings on the possibility of war with Germany. She was also tasked, it has been suggested, with photographing sensitive documentation obtained clandestinely from the unsuspecting officers while their attention was diverted – presumably by her noted feminine charms. While there appear to be records to confirm that Vera did indeed stay with the Duchess – in Baker Street – the suggestion that all this happened in the summer of 1939 seems at odds with another of the headline-grabbing theories linked to this most enigmatic of women.

MI5 files released in 2000 revealed that, shortly before the war in the summer of 1939, Vera gave birth to a son. The hitherto secret documents suggested that the child was born in England and was sent soon afterwards to an orphanage in Essex.

So, if Vera had been dispatched to London in the pre-war months of 1939, she must either have travelled to England already pregnant or she arrived at the start of the year and almost immediately conceived. As those (Kluiters and Verhoeyen among them) who insist on 1939 as the year of her visit suggest that she did not actually reach London until June, the former is probably the more likely explanation. The identity of the child's father has never been publicly revealed. There are, of course, many theories. One that has gathered momentum in recent years is that the father was a high-ranking member of the British establishment. This again brings into question the precise timing of Vera's pre-war mission. According to some historians, it might also help to explain her ultimate fate. It is an aspect of Vera's story that can conveniently be put to one side for the moment. If she really was in London pre-war, there is no real evidence that she succeeded in extracting anything of a sensitive nature from the RAF officers (or anyone else) she may or may not have befriended which transcended the confines of the tearoom (or bedroom). Vera's pre-war spying mission – or maybe missions? – to the UK is or are another murky mystery.

This does not, however, apply to her next venture in Britain – not to the first part of it, anyway. Vera's return in September 1940 has been well chronicled. It is as hard to believe as the rest of her life story but, unlike the earlier chapters of the tale, its authenticity is verifiable. The much written about events which coincided with Dorothy O'Grady's own rise to notoriety in the latter months of 1940 are illuminated with the clarity of recall by those who were witness to them.

It stands as one of the most eccentric, poorly planned and badly executed spying missions of the Second World War, an operation that ended in abject failure, the death of two agents – and the mystery that envelopes Vera Schalburg to this day and may link her to the story of Dorothy O'Grady beyond the realms of pure coincidence. Essentially, the plan was to send Vera back to the UK, this time with male Abwehr colleagues, for intelligence gathering tasks at the heart of Western Europe's last remaining bastion of resistance against the Nazi menace.

The mission was the brainchild of the high-ranking and much respected Abwehr officer Erwin von Lahousen. Entrusted by him to lead the high-risk mission was Hilmar Dierks, who would be accompanied by Vera, his mistress, and fellow agents Robert Petter, a skilled wireless operator born in the Swiss city of Zurich, and Karl Drücke, another of the stars of Dierks' spying coterie in Hamburg. Convoluted cover stories, it was hoped, would enable the agents to operate safely and to maximum effect once they were safely installed on British soil. Unfortunately for Generalleutnant Lahousen and the Abwehr, things started to go disastrously wrong before the mission had left the soil of Germany.[7,8]

On 2 September, the day before they were due to leave for the UK, the four agents took time off from their preparations for a night out in Hamburg – a celebratory send-off to the mission. The assumption has always been that their alcohol consumption that night was far from moderate. With Hilmar Dierks at the wheel, they travelled by car back to their hotel accommodation. The vehicle overturned. All but Dierks escaped with relatively minor injuries, but for the mission chief, a man who had served Germany's secret service agencies with distinction since 1914, there was to be no escape. The car crash claimed his life.

The tragic loss of such a key figure should probably have persuaded the Abwehr to abort the mission. They decided not to. After a three-week delay, a man short and apparently still bearing visible evidence of their injuries from the crash, Schalburg, Petter and Drücke were on their way to occupied Norway on the first leg of their hazardous journey. Dierks' death had deprived Vera not only of her mission chief but also her lover. It seems Karl Drücke may have been able to alleviate her distress – according to some researchers they had 'fallen in love'. Whatever her personal turmoil, Vera appears to have adopted the leader's role. The Abwehr had decreed that in London she would play the part of Vera Erikson, a Danish national and, true to form, the niece of an Italian countess living in Kensington with a string of influential British contacts. Drucke would travel as Francois de Deeker, a French refugee who had arrived in the UK from Belgium, while Petter would assume the identity of Werner Heinrich Walti, a Swiss subject. Their forged ID would show them living at addresses in Paddington – Sussex Place for Vera and Sussex Gardens for the men.[9]

The plan was to convey the trio in a flying boat from Stavanger to a point just off the north-east coast of Scotland. There they would be taken to the shore in a rubber dinghy – accompanied by three English bicycles liberated from the British Consul in Bergen. The cycles would provide their onward transport all the way to London, more than 600 miles to the south! That the Abwehr could have come up with such a ludicrous idea speaks volumes for the total inadequacy of their mission planning. It was scuppered. literally, before it could be set in motion. The aircraft did succeed, after two attempts were thwarted by unfavourable weather conditions, in dropping the agents, on the night of 29 September, off Gollachy, between Buckie and Portgordon on the Moray Firth coast. The trio had rehearsed launching the inflatable dinghy from the flying boat while in Norway and this part of the operation also went according to plan.

But the sea was choppy. The three bicycles either missed the dinghy altogether while being lowered from the flying boat or were swept overboard soon after 'landing' – accounts vary – but the outcome was the same. The spies' intended means of transport to London plunged to the seabed and never made it ashore. The agents *did* make it to dry land. Unhappily for them, they were far from dry themselves thanks to the turbulent sea. This was not going to help their cause. What happened next is enshrined in the folklore of this out-of-the-way corner of the Scottish mainland's far north. It was, and will probably always remain, the area's foremost claim to fame, an episode recalled locally in the minutest of detail.

With 'plan A' thwarted, the hapless agents made two key decisions as they stood, bedraggled and miserable, on the remote shoreline – to split up and then to travel by train to London. Petter set off eastwards for the town of Buckie while Schalburg and Drücke trudged west to Portgordon village. Both places had stations on the Moray Coast Railway, effectively a loop line to the north of – and connected to it at both ends – the London & North Eastern Railway's main line between Inverness and Aberdeen, and thence south across the English border.

Carrying a large suitcase and two smaller bags, Vera Schalburg and Karl Drücke reached Portgordon station around 7.30 a.m. The fact that they were strangers arriving in wartime on a very local branch line was enough in itself to arouse the suspicions of the railway staff – stationmaster John Donald and porter John Geddes. The portends therefore were already bleak when Vera spoke – to ask the name of the station. The platform name boards, as was the case at virtually all other stations on the national rail network, had been removed or painted over for security reasons, but the strangers' obvious ignorance of where they were was bound to heighten the unease of Donald and Geddes.

Drücke then pointed to a timetable on the wall. Inexplicably, he indicated the station at Forres, west of Elgin on the route to Inverness, mispronouncing it as 'Forest'. Opening his wallet, crammed full of banknotes, he laid far too much money on the ticket office counter for the cost of the two third-class single tickets Donald assumed he wanted. At this point the stationmaster noticed that the bottom of Drücke's trousers were soaking wet, as were his companion's stockings and shoes. Unhelpfully for the spies, it was a dry morning at Portgordon.

With an instruction to Geddes to 'keep them talking', stationmaster Donald telephoned the local policeman, PC Bob Grieve, in Portgordon's Stewart Street. The constable hot-footed it to the railway station, arriving within ten minutes. If Schalburg and Drücke thought they might be in trouble – and they could hardly have failed to – they had lost their chance to escape the clutches of the law.

Grieve asked to see the couple's identity cards. Once again the Abwehr planners had let down their spies – the cards were poor imitations of the real thing. Crucially, the handwritten details had clearly been entered in a tell-tale continental European style and neither card carried the immigration stamp that would have been expected on the ID of people claiming, as they were, to be refugees. PC Grieve had what he needed. He asked the pair to accompany him to the police station. Did they still think they could convince the local police that they were harmless? It seems so. They went dutifully with the constable to Stewart Street. Once there, Grieve telephoned Inspector John Simpson at Buckie to report the incident. Rather than lock up the pair in the cells, he invited them into the police house where his wife made a cup of tea for Vera as she sat in the sitting room. This domestic interlude was soon interrupted by the arrival by car of Simpson. The inspector asked Drücke to identify himself. 'He cannot speak English,' said Vera before her colleague had the opportunity to reply.

It went from bad to worse for the agents when Simpson, suspecting Drücke might be armed, searched his clothes – and found a box with nineteen rounds of revolver ammunition. The inspector turned his attention to Schalburg. Having given Vera Erikson as her name, she told him that she was 27 (thus giving rise to the probable, but far from certain, notion that she was born in December 1912), a widow and a Danish subject who originated from Siberia. Asked to prove it, she produced once again the false National Registration Card issued by her Abwehr handlers. Drücke now did the same, showing Simpson his registration card in the name of Francois de Deeker. The inspector confirmed for himself what Grieve had told him about the dubious nature of the ID. Soon, the pair were on their way to the more secure surrounds of the police station in Buckie. John Simpson was now in little doubt that enemy agents had landed in his patch.

Asked at Buckie what she and Drücke had been doing in Portgordon, and how they had got there, Vera said they had travelled down in a small boat from Bergen – she named both the vessel and its captain – and had stayed the night at an hotel in Banff, a coastal town some 20 miles to the east. They had taken a taxi that morning to within a mile of Portgordon, then walked the rest of the way to the station. Inspector Simpson must have listened to this with incredulity. Banff had its own railway station so there was little, if any, point to such a car ride – and why would a taxi drop them off a mile or so from the station they were supposedly making for? Simpson wasn't taken in by any of this.

Cover stories by then had themselves become pointless. The inspector had ordered a thorough search of the pair's possessions, their baggage included. What it revealed shot away any remaining pretence that Schalburg and Drücke were harmless refugees. Among other, more easily explained, items Drücke was found to be carrying a pocket knife and a torch clearly marked 'Made in Bohemia'. Years later, John Simpson would describe melodramatically how he then 'burst open' Drücke's suitcase. It might as well have been emblazoned with the letters 'SPY'. Among the choicest of the contents were a small Mauser pistol loaded with six rounds of ammunition, a wireless transmitter set, three small and two large batteries, two wrapped radio valves, a voltmeter, headphones, a Morse tapping key, a cardboard disc coding device, a three-way plug with wiring and, on a sheet of paper, a list of RAF bases in Britain. Drücke's leather wallet contained

£327 in Bank of England notes – a very significant sum of money in 1940 – while Vera Schalburg's purse held another £72. All this was damning enough, though some say it was the discovery in Drücke's possession of a half-eaten German sausage, unobtainable in the UK, which convinced Inspector Simpson that the agents had set off from enemy territory.

The evidence continued to pile up. At 11.45 a.m. the Buckie coastguard spotted something floating in the sea about 0.25 miles offshore. He and the harbourmaster set out to retrieve the object – revealed as the pair of bellows used to inflate the spies' rubber dinghy. The dinghy itself, rolled up and abandoned by the careless Nazi agents, was soon located a short distance further out. But what had happened to the third occupant of the craft, Robert Petter?

He had done rather better than his colleagues. Possibly by chance, after leaving the others he had found himself at Buckpool station, a mile short of Buckie. It was 6.50 a.m. – and he had just missed the train to Aberdeen. It would be three hours before the next departure south from the Moray coast. Either to allay suspicion or simply to kill time, Petter opted to walk on to Buckie and board the train there. He reached the town's station around 7.45 a.m., bought a ticket to Edinburgh and waited for the 9.58 a.m. departure which would take him on the first leg of his journey as far as Aberdeen. Nothing happened to impede his exit from the firth but, unsurprisingly, Petter's presence on the Banff branch line had been noted. When the police, with two spies already in custody, began making enquiries in the belief that others might also have landed, they were quickly on his trail.[10]

Aberdeen police confirmed that a man matching Petter's description had boarded the 1 p.m. train to Edinburgh. If he felt that luck was on his side when his journey to the Scottish capital passed without serious incident – an ID check at Dundee apparently revealing nothing suspicious – his confidence must have taken a knock when he alighted at Edinburgh Waverley station at 4.30 p.m. and was told the next departure south to London would not be until 10 p.m. Petter was advised to deposit his obviously laden suitcase in a left luggage office and return for it in plenty of time for his train. He followed the advice, walking into Princes Street where he had a shave, ate a meal and strolled off to a nearby cinema. By this time, news had filtered through to Edinburgh police that Petter had travelled down to Waverley on the train from the north. Arriving too late at the station to catch him there, the Scottish Special Branch orchestrated a search of the city's streets, hotels, hostels, bars and restaurants. Petter evaded the net.

However, enquiries at the station had revealed the whereabouts of his suitcase, sharp-eyes officers noticing a whitish 'tide mark' suggesting it had been standing recently in sea water. The case was opened and its contents noted before it was returned to storage. Petter had been carrying a wireless transmitter set, its German manufacture obvious. When he returned for the case the police were waiting for him. Famously, he was overcome by a small man disguised as a railway porter – the legendary Scottish policeman William 'Wee Willie' Merrilees, who had led the hunt. While in the hands of Merrilees' men, Petter, who had already unsuccessfully attempted to use an automatic pistol, pulled a knife from his pocket. According to Wee Willie's 1966 autobiography, it was his police force's first exposure to a flick-knife. 'We were just in time to prevent him using the gleaming blade,' he wrote. At police HQ, Petter's baggage was searched. Another haul of spying paraphernalia was found. Robert Petter spoke good English but there was no chance of him talking his way out of this.[11]

Betrayed by desperately poor Abwehr groundwork and outwitted by solid Scottish policing, Schalburg, Drücke and Petter finally made it to London, though the circumstances surrounding their arrival there in police custody could not have been more different to those envisaged by an optimistic Lahousen in Germany. From this point the story divides two ways, one path leading into stark, terrible and unquestionable hard facts, the other into deep mystery.

The Special Branch handed over the trio for interrogation by MI5. This was led by Lt. Colonel Hinchley Cooke, who by then also had on his hands the bothersome matter of what to make of Dorothy O'Grady. It seems clear from the available evidence that Drücke and Petter said very little to the Security Service, Petter denying any knowledge of his two fellow spies throughout the questioning. Undoubtedly, Hinchley Cooke and his colleagues attempted to 'turn' the men in the interests of Britain. Neither bowed to the pressure. Their refusal to betray Germany by working as double agents could have but one consequence. Drücke (35) and Petter (25 – prosecuted in the name of Werner Walti) signed statements in March 1941 and were committed under the Treachery Act to appear before a secret Old Bailey trial the following June. The evidence against them was overwhelming. The jury retired for only a few minutes before returning guilty verdicts. The appeals process made no difference. On 6 August they were hanged by Albert Pierrepoint at Wandsworth prison.

To this day, no official explanation has been provided for the absence of Vera Schalburg in the Old Bailey dock alongside her male Abwehr colleagues. The documents released by the government in 2000 sparked a flurry of speculation that Vera's complicated sex life may have been the reason she escaped prosecution and the gallows. The question was asked: had a prominent British establishment figure fathered the child born to Vera in 1939? And, if so, had this in itself been enough to save her life? 'It is entirely speculative,' Portgordon historian Dr Peter Reid told the national press from his home at the village's former police station in October 2000, 'but her brief was to infiltrate prominent society. It's quite plausible that she did take one of her liaisons to its natural conclusion, although I don't think we will ever know the identity of the father.' He added. 'Being the mother of a British subject with perhaps an important father, may have played a major part in the decision not to put her on trial.'

The MI5 files released to the Public Record Office revealed that Vera asked to see her son following her arrest in 1940 and it seems the boy may have been bought from Essex to visit her. The unanswered question is – what was Vera's status at the time? The 'new' information formed part of a compendium of papers relating to female wartime internees – a clear indication that Vera was simply interned for the remainder of the war and then sent 'home' to Germany. But there is compelling evidence that it was not as clear-cut as that, evidence that suggests Vera's active wartime involvement was far from over in October 1940.

Speculation that Vera was always a British agent, double-crossing the Abwehr from the start, is not borne out by what is known of her interrogation in the UK. Publication in 2005 of the wartime diaries compiled by MI5's Guy Liddell revealed several references to an obviously distressed Vera in the early part of October. On the 7th, a week after her capture, Liddell noted that she 'shows signs of going on hunger strike. She has been moved to Holloway prison.' (Where Dorothy O'Grady was awaiting her committal hearing at Ryde, making this the first occasion the two women were under the same roof at the same time.) A subsequent diary reference, on 9 October, makes clear that Vera had started to talk. Under interrogation she had admitted that 'before the war she had worked as a spy in Paris for the Soviet military intelligence service, the GRU'.

From this point on it is possible to construct a convincing case that, unlike Karl Drücke and Robert Petter, Vera *did* agree to work for Britain against her former employers. She was not German; there is little to suggest she had any particular affinity with the Nazi regime, on whose behalf she had apparently agreed to become a spy for reasons of personal, rather than political, interest. Vera was also, if the accounts of her pre-war life are to be believed, accustomed to changing sides in the espionage game. Clues have emerged in recent years from the release of previously hidden information to support the view that she was used by British intelligence in a role that would enable her to remain in the UK.

Another interpretation is that, despite prolonged efforts on the part of MI5 to secure her services for Britain, she declined the opportunity, a decision that would usually have produced the direst of consequences for a captured enemy agent.

If she *did* succumb to MI5's pressure, the precise nature of what she did following the unravelling of the Abwehr's maladroit mission in the north of Scotland is another aspect of Vera's story that is still shrouded in mystery. That the focus has fallen on Aylesbury prison is an intriguing twist, for it is there that the stories of Dorothy O'Grady and Vera Schalburg appear to collide. Did they meet there? Were they in some way linked? And how did MI5 regard them both in 1941–42 as they adjusted in their distinctively separate ways to life in a controlled environment? One thing is certain: Britain's wartime intelligence chiefs were destined to take a very keen interest in the goings-on at Aylesbury prison.

# Notes

1   August Theodor Schalburg and Jelena Startiskaja von Siemandvska have been put forward as the names of both Vera's and Christian's parents, the accompanying suggestion being that Jelena's aristocratic family owned large estates in Ukraine. Christian's birthplace in 1906 was Zmeinogorsk in Russia.

2   Ballets Russes (Russian Ballets) was an itinerant ballet company, which performed in many countries between 1909 and 1929. Following the 1917 Revolution in Russia, the company's younger dancers were drawn, like Vera, from those trained in Paris and living there within the city's community of Russian exiles.

3   Hard drugs like cocaine had become increasingly popular by the 1930s in many parts of Europe, most notably in the vice-ridden German city of Berlin where recreational drug use was relatively common.

4   According to some sources, Vera's alleged drug addiction was still an issue when she arrived on her ill-fated mission to the UK on 30 September 1940. As noted, the photographs taken of her the next day depict a woman apparently suffering from a lack of sleep. The suggestion is that she was also coming down from a drugs fix administered by her Abwehr handlers en route to the north-east coast of Scotland.

5   Kluiters and Verhoeyen's account of Vera's story features in their internet collaboration: *An International Spymaster and Mystery Man – Abwehr officer Hilmar J. Dierks (1889–1940) and his agents.*

6   In 1939 Christian von Shalburg was appointed to head Denmark's far-Right National Socialist Workers' Party's youth section. He volunteered the same year to fight against the Soviet Union in the Finnish Winter War (1939–40) and was not in Denmark when the country was occupied by the Germans

in April 1940. Although distressed by his nation's capitulation, he joined the Waffen-SS and served on the staff of the Wiking Division during Operation Barbarossa, Germany's invasion of the USSR in June 1941, gaining the Iron Cross. His Nazi ideology made him an ideal choice for later command roles with the Frikorps Danmark (Danish Free Corps) until his death in June 1942 on active service.

7  Erwin von Lahousen (1897–1955), a member of an aristocratic Austrian family, worked for his country's counter-intelligence service before its absorption by the Abwehr at the time of the Anschluss (union with Germany) in 1938. Never comfortable with Nazi doctrine, he became a prominent member of the anti-Hitler 'resistance' movement and, following his transfer to the Eastern Front in 1943, later gave evidence of German atrocities in that sector of the war when he was called as a key witness for the prosecution at the Nuremburg War Crimes Trials of Hermann Goering and other prominent Nazi figures.

8  Drücke's surname is sometimes referred to as Drügge, though he used the former spelling during interrogation.

9  According to some sources, Vera's 1940 mission to England carried an enhanced risk because she had already been 'flagged up' as a possible spy during an MI5 interrogation of female Nazi agent Josephine Eriksson (real surname Karpp) who had been intercepted in December 1939 as she attempted to leave Gravesend for Rotterdam. The incident was linked, it is said, to Vera's pre-war stay in London, though the sources suggest that Vera had not aroused any significant suspicion while she was in the capital.

10  Having played a large role in the story of the German spies' capture, the local rail network on the Moray coast slipped back into quiet obscurity. By 1968 it had fallen victim to the infamous Beeching axe.

11  Wee Willie's recollections of Petter's arrest were featured in *The Short Arm of the Law: The Memoirs of William Merrilees OBE* (London: John Long, 1966).

# 11

# Keeping Watch on a Spy Doing Time

As a woman convicted of wartime treachery who had wriggled free of the hangman's noose on the technicalities of legal argument, Dorothy O'Grady was assured of a special status when she arrived at Aylesbury in February 1941 to begin her prison sentence. She was a 'star' prisoner and would several times be described as such in reports from the jail over the months and years that followed. She wasted little time in playing up to the role of a leading lady. Trouble and O'Grady were destined to go hand-in-hand in the Buckinghamshire prison.

As early as 29 April, Mary Size, Aylesbury's governor, was writing to the prison commissioners with the first of many references to the troublesome inmate. Dorothy O'Grady, she remarked:

is trying to spread anti-British propaganda whenever she gets the chance. The majority of the women take no notice of her but a few of the worse types of prisoner ... walk with her at exercise. The officers and I are alive to the danger and watch her closely, but so far there has been no occurrence on which a report could be formulated against her. She has threatened suicide but has made no attempt to carry out the threat.[1]

A few months later, O'Grady, the convicted spy, became the target herself for some internal intelligence gathering within the Aylesbury prison walls. Writing on 29 August 1941 to W.H. Waddams at the Prison Commission, Mary Size reported:

> Some weeks ago, a convict, de Trafford, who is friendly with O'Grady, gave me some information which I thought might be useful to MI5. I asked her to write down the conversations [with O'Grady] verbatim as far as she could remember them. I gave her an exercise book, into which she has put the correspondence up to date. I am submitting the notes to you for your advice.

Waddams forwarded Miss Size's letter and the exercise book to the Home Office, which had already received copies of statements made by Dorothy while awaiting her trial. Evidently, he had posted the letter for he was told that, in future, any further material of this kind should be sent instead by 'internal communications'. Thus was set in train a flow of de Trafford's notes on her subsequent conversations with O'Grady, scribbled down in the exercise books provided for the purpose by Mary Size. There is no indication that O'Grady knew, or suspected, that she was being so closely monitored by a fellow inmate and, through her, the Home Office, but, given her previous behaviour, it is tempting to conclude that, *had* she known, she would probably not have been displeased.

Dorothy was certainly not concerned with keeping anything resembling a low profile. On the morning of 19 December she created panic in the prison when, having been let out of her cell after lock-up, she wandered off from the landing on which she was confined and was outside before anxious staff caught up with her.

As for de Trafford – whose first name and reason for imprisonment were not disclosed in the correspondence – it seems clear that she was relishing her role as prison informer. Not only did she continue to furnish the Home Office and MI5 with copious notes on her dialogue with O'Grady, she also provided accounts of conversations with several other prisoners, including Anna Wolkoff. On New Year's Eve 1941

Waddams told the governor the de Trafford notes 'have proved of some interest' and suggested that Miss Size 'unobtrusively encourages the continuance of the conversations and records' while at the same time providing her views on 'de Trafford's reliability and judgment'.[2]

The Aylesbury governor told him that:

> generally speaking, de Trafford is not altogether reliable, but I believe she is out to help the country in any way she can, and the idea of reporting these conversations emanates from her desire to help. She has subscribed regularly from her wages to the Red Cross Fund since we introduced it. Her subscription for 1941 is 13/9 ... Her loyalty appears to be genuine.

The fact that de Trafford had donated nearly 14*s* (70p), a significant sum in 1941, to the Red Cross was apparently not enough to convince Waddams, nor the Home Office, of her reliability as an informant. They needed to be sure. De Trafford's notes had, it seems, indicated strongly Dorothy O'Grady's repeated assertion that she was not allowing her imprisonment to get in the way of her contact with, and supply of information to, the enemy. On 10 January 1942 Mary Size was asked by Waddams for an elaboration of de Trafford's reliability as a source 'and for enlargement on points made in the notes'.

Frustratingly, the notes in question have been excluded from the archived papers. It is, however, clear from the documents that have been released for public inspection that Waddams had heard from the Home Office that they wanted Miss Size's response to 'O'Grady's reported statements about her methods of getting messages in and out [of the prison], and the other prisoners etc alleged to be implicated in the matter'. Implicated by whom? O'Grady or de Trafford? Or both? There is no way of telling from the available archived material.

Under pressure from Home Office staff, who were clearly being prompted by MI5, Governor Size admitted she could not vouch for the veracity of de Trafford's notes but reiterated that the prisoner's loyalty 'appears to be genuine'. She added that she and her officers were 'carefully watching' O'Grady's alleged 'trafficking confederates'.

It was an unsettling response from the jail. On the face of it, prisoner O'Grady was continuing to pose a serious security risk at the start of 1942. MI5 clearly felt they could afford to take no chances.

The perception at the Security Service of Dorothy O'Grady is as interesting as it is conflicting. On the one hand we have the seemingly scathing dismissal of her spying credentials offered by Guy Liddell. On the other there is the evidence of MI5's obvious desire to keep a close watch on her at Aylesbury and record her dialogue with fellow prisoners, though it is unclear whether it was Dorothy herself or the women she and de Trafford were apparently 'fingering' as potential traitors who most interested the men running Britain's intelligence service.

MI5 needed more reliable help from inside the Buckinghamshire prison. Did they consider 'planting' someone who could infiltrate the jail and report back directly to them on the realities of the threat flagged up in prisoner de Trafford's copious notes? Is it possible that they turned to Vera Schalburg? Was this part of a covert role she played for the Security Service after she was successfully turned?

The O'Grady archives unsurprisingly make no reference to Vera Schalburg, implied or otherwise. In order to pursue the possibility of an MI5 link it is necessary to look elsewhere among the burgeoning pile of once secret, but now publicly available, records relating to wartime British intelligence and security issues.

Unlikely as it may seem, the starting point for this process is a biography, published in 1973, of the actor and playwright Peter Ustinov's father, Jona von Ustinov. In this book his widow, Nadia Benois, reveals how Jona's dislike of the name he was given led to him always being know to family and friends as Klop. It remains a whimsical mystery why he should have adopted the Russian word for a bedbug, but this apparently trivial revelation would later prove hugely significant when wartime MI5 files were released to The National Archives.[3]

Klop Ustinov, who had a Russian father and a German mother, had served with distinction in the German army during the First World War, winning the Iron Cross. He later moved to London to work as a journalist with what became known as the German News Agency, before falling out of favour with the Nazi regime through his refusal in 1935 to prove Aryan descent. His profound disenchantment with the political situation in Germany led to his recruitment in London as a British intelligence officer who was given the MI5 code name U35. As such, he was prominently involved in the Double-Cross System and its hugely successful turning of captured German spies to work in the British interest.[4]

It is therefore easy to link references to 'Klop' in archives and related publications to agent U35 Ustinov – and there is no shortage of these. Guy Liddell's diary entry for 19 December 1941 is particularly significant in the context of a possible Aylesbury connection between Vera Schalburg (usually referred to as Vera Eriksson by Liddell) and MI5's unease about Dorothy O'Grady: 'I had a discussion ... with Klop about Vera Eriksson. He is quite ready to have her but would welcome the assistance of one of T. A. Robertson's Field Security Policemen. He does not wish to see Vera until she arrives at his house.'

It is unclear why Ustinov felt he needed the help of the Field Security wing of the Royal Military Police, but Liddell's diary entry at least provides the first clear indication that Vera was being lined up by MI5 at the end of 1941 for a covert assignment. A month later, on 29 January 1942, Liddell noted, 'We propose to get Vera Eriksson to Aylesbury prison on Sunday and to Klop's on Tuesday.'

Liddell gave no further details, nor did he refer in either of these two diary entries to Vera's whereabouts throughout 1941, but now, early in 1942, she was about to be sent to HMP Aylesbury – where Dorothy O'Grady's wild talk, no doubt aided and abetted by the note-taking de Trafford, was creating a huge stir.

Was this merely a switch of secure accommodation? A transfer from one prison to another while Klop Ustinov continued to try his best to recruit Vera's services? There are many who hold to this view, though Aylesbury's wartime internees were not usually allowed out in midweek for a spot of lunch in London!

It cannot be ruled out – but neither can the possibility that MI5 were dispatching Vera to the jail as a spy already recruited to gather information. If so, it is tempting to speculate in what guise they were sending her. If it was as a prisoner, the midweek leave aspect remains unfathomable. Was she instead to masquerade as some kind of official visitor? There are no firm clues to help determine this. It can, however, probably be assumed that any willingness on Vera's part to carry out her mission, if that's what it was, at Aylesbury was adversely affected a few days later when she was finally told that Karl Drücke and Robert Petter, the two fellow spies who had accompanied her on that shambolic spying mission to Britain, had been hanged neatly six months earlier.

'Vera Eriksson was told by Edward Hinchley Cooke about her proposed move,' Guy Liddell recorded on 1 February. 'She asked what had happened to Drücke and Walti [Petter] and was much concerned to hear that they had been executed.'

If she had not already started work for MI5, Vera was clearly actively involved within the next five days. On 6 February Liddell noted, 'It seems that the Vera Eriksson case is going on well. The lady is doing her best to help though it seems likely that she has not got a very intimate knowledge of the organisation.'

To the present-day reader this is clearly open to interpretation. What type of organisation was Liddell referring to? Some sort of formal grouping posing an apparent threat to British security, perhaps? Or might it have been the perceived organisation of trafficking messages to the enemy from inside the walls of Aylesbury prison? Caution needs to be exercised in attempting to make the sketchy information provided by Liddell's now cryptic diary jottings fit within the theory of a possible link at the jail between Vera and Dorothy. Liddell's notes do not, of course, amount to proof. Neither do they rule out that possibility.

On 9 February Liddell recorded dining with Klop Ustinov when 'Vera Eriksson's case' was discussed. Klop, he noted, 'has got a number of interesting details, but his picture is not yet complete. He is quite convinced that Vera is doing her best.' Just one week later, on 16 February, came Liddell's final references to Vera. 'I dined with Klop who gave us an account of Vera Eriksson, who has gone back to Aylesbury prison. She has I think done her best for us.'[5]

It seems clear that Vera spent most, if not all, of this period in early February 1942 at Ustinov's London home. Evidently, she had enjoyed herself there. On 15 February, after leaving him and his wife for the last time, she had sent Klop a brief letter of thanks, now preserved among the archives: 'I have been very happy staying with you both and I hope the time will come when we shall meet again under more normal circumstances.' The note was informally signed 'Vera' to round off this mysterious episode – and bring to an end all recorded verifiable references to 'the beautiful spy'. She is never mentioned again in the records.

How long she remained at Aylesbury, and in precisely what capacity, is unknown. If her MI5 assignment was connected in any way with Dorothy O'Grady, and this remains a tantalising possibility, it seems to have come to an end in mid-February 1942 – and it has to be admitted that, if she *was* spying at the jail, Vera was given very little time to do so between arriving there on a Sunday and visiting Ustinov only two days later. The case is still open to question.

Remarkably, however, Aylesbury prison was not the final apparent connection between the two women. As previously noted, Vera's post-war history, as interpreted by some of her many devotees, suggests there could be a further link.[6]

Several researchers adhere to the view that, rather than being returned to Germany at the end of the war, Vera was in fact given a new identity and spent the rest of her life quietly in southern England, where she died in 1993. The evidence is far from conclusive but the story was elevated beyond the realms of rumour, supposition and fantasy in 1975 when her sister-in-law, Helle von Bulow, the widow of Vera's brother, Christian von Schalburg, told in an interview of being in regular contact by letter with Vera. Released after wartime internment, she added, Vera *had* been allowed to stay in England, remaining in the south where she married and later became both a mother and grandmother. This is by some distance the most creditable evidence in support of the theory that Vera did not leave the UK. If true, where precisely did she live?

The suggestion that it was the Isle of Wight is widely held, and not merely in the UK. Proving it is another matter. In 1976 the quarterly magazine *After the Battle* devoted an entire issue to the story of German spies in Britain which naturally included extensive coverage of Vera's story. In a post-script editor Winston G. Ramsey told his readers that, after the war, when Erwin von Lahousen, the Abwehr officer who so catastrophically masterminded Vera's spying mission to the UK, was in a British internment camp at Bad Nenndorf, near Hanover, Lower Saxony, he was interviewed by an unnamed (though Ramsey suggested this might have been Edward Hinchley Cooke) British colonel:

> Answering a question from Lahousen, the colonel was recorded as saying, 'You're wondering what happened to Vera, the beautiful spy, as we called her. Well, you're absolutely right. She came over to us. If you ever want to see her again, well I would have a look around the Isle of Wight. I think you might find her there – with another name of course – and nobody there has the slightest idea of her background' ...

Ramsey added, rather hopefully, 'If Vera reads this story, or sees the film we have made about her, the editor, after spending so long reviewing her story, would be thrilled to hear from her – wherever she now happens to be.' There is no record that Vera ever did get in touch with him.

Winson Ramsey did not reveal his source for the Isle of Wight link to Vera, but it has been picked up by many since the article appeared in 1976 and her post-war residency on the island is often today related as a fact. It may be so but no real proof has ever emerged. If she did settle down on the isle, it would not take too much of a leap in imagination to suggest she might well have met up with Dorothy O'Grady, with whom she was most certainly at the same prisons in wartime.[7]

In all her many interviews, Dorothy never referred to Vera as a near-neighbour. Indeed, she made no reference at all to her, despite the certainty of their shared prison occupancy. Unless, that is, Vera Schalburg adopted the disguise of an eastern European aristocrat (and it would have been entirely in keeping with what is known of her life as a spy) when she was sent to Aylesbury prison in February 1942. Could she have been masquerading there as the 'haughty-taughty Russian countess' O'Grady had somewhat disdainfully mentioned in the 1980s? 'She never spoke to us ... we never knew why she was there,' Dorothy had said.

Whether or not Vera was briefly used by MI5 in February 1942 in their frantic bid to monitor the apparent security risk fuelled by Dorothy at Aylesbury, there is no doubt that the Home Office was keeping up the pressure on Mary Size for information. Maybe the strain proved too much for the governor. During that month she had left the prison on extended sick leave. Now the pressure fell on her deputy, a Miss King, who was bombarded with demands from the Home Office – relayed by W.H. Waddams – for particulars about 'different persons mentioned in the [de Trafford] notes' and for 'relevant observations – e.g. O'Grady's alleged determination to pass information to her husband at a "closed" visit'. Clearly, Miss King was flummoxed. Waddams had to tell his impatient Home Office contacts early in March that the governor's deputy was 'not capable' of providing explanatory notes on the scale required by the Security Service.[8]

The saga of the de Trafford notes rumbled on to no real effect as the enthusiastic prison informer continued to broaden her target sights, compiling notes on an increasingly lengthy list of fellow inmates and, to the evident frustration of the Home Office and MI5, straying widely from her original quarry. An intriguing handwritten, but unsigned, note, now in the archived file, urged all concerned that no credence should be given to de Trafford's reports as she was 'the biggest liar and false pretender who has passed through my hands'. Before long, the prison authorities were beginning seriously to wonder whether such a description could equally be applied to Dorothy O'Grady herself.

As she would years later tell the *Sunday Express*'s Sidney Rodin, she had written a letter to her husband and requested that it be forwarded to him. Naturally, the contents were read at the prison and a copy was then passed by Waddams at the Prison Commission to the Home

Office. It was understood, said Waddams in his accompanying note, that Vincent O'Grady had reproached his wife 'for her actions which led to her conviction'. This, he said, had 'rather upset O'Grady who wishes to put herself right in the eyes of her husband by saying that the whole case against her was built up on misapprehension of the facts'.

Dorothy had strutted gleefully around the prison spouting anti-British cant to anyone who cared to listen. She had openly boasted of feeding the enemy with information from within the prison confines. She had proudly worn 'home-made' swastika emblems, talked of the inevitability of German victory. She was a 'star' prisoner and she had lived up to the billing – Dorothy O'Grady, Nazi spy.

Yet, in that March 1942 letter to the reproachful Vincent, for the first time since her arrest, she was apparently going out of her way to assert that the image of her as a committed enemy agent, one she had worked so hard to promote, was actually well wide of the mark. That letter is not among the archives. It is thus impossible to say if what Dorothy told her husband amounted to a renewed blanket denial of the charges against her or an assurance that, while she *had* committed the crimes that had landed her in jail, this did not in itself make her a Nazi-leaning traitor. If the latter was the case, it would have been interesting to know just how she interpreted her wartime activities for her bemused husband. Whatever she wrote to him, it clearly did not fit with her self-crafted prison persona.

If, as seems likely, the letter was interpreted initially by the authorities merely as a means of assuaging Vincent, Dorothy's subsequent behaviour may have changed their minds. During the remainder of 1942 and throughout 1943 the archived documents suggest she had finally adopted a relatively low prison profile – which tallies in broad terms with her own accounts of the mid-war years.

There was, however, some concern for her heath in October 1942. The prison's medical officer reported that she was suffering from a fibroid growth of the uterus, a common condition usually affecting women at the mid and late reproductive stages. While symptom-free at the time of diagnosis, the MO added that, the fibroid was increasing in size and would soon require operative intervention. The operation was duly carried out in February 1943. Dorothy was transferred to a hospital outside the prison for a hysterectomy. There were no complications and her general health was later said to have benefited as a result.

But this assessment by the medical officer did not tell the full story. It related solely to her *physical* condition. Her mental state was another matter altogether. It was soon to dominate the story of Dorothy O'Grady's mid-term years at Aylesbury. That period of her imprisonment was, and is, crucial to a full understanding of the complex forces which drove Dorothy on the road to infamy.

# Notes

1　Evidently, Dorothy O'Grady's anti-British rhetoric in prison had spread beyond the walls of the jail. Mary Size's report to the Prison Commission was in response to an alert from the police in Reigate, Surrey. They had been approached by Louise Howard, a prisoner recently released from Aylesbury, expressing alarm at O'Grady's pro-German rants. While Howard had exaggerated her prison association with 'the spy', her police statement added to the pressure on the governor to keep a close watch on Dorothy.

2　The Aylesbury prison informant de Trafford remains a shadowy figure in Dorothy O'Grady's story, not least because her first name and the reason for detaining her in the prison were never revealed in the copious correspondence that passed between Governor Mary Size and the Home Office. The de Trafford family name is among the most illustrious in Lancashire, particularly associated with the city of Manchester.

3　Ustinov, Nadia B. and Peter, *Klop and the Ustinov Family* (Okpaku Communications, 1973).

4　Klop Ustinov's father was Baron Plato Grigorievich Ustinov (1840–1918), a Russian-born aristocrat, and his mother was Magdalena Hall, from the German town of Magdala (1868–1945). The couple were married in 1889. Magdalena's mother was Katharina Hall (1850–1932), who had Ethiopian descent. Klop knew that his grandmother's Ethiopian origins would not satisfy the strict Nazi Aryan racial criteria.

5　Liddell added a fascinating 'post-script' about Vera and her doomed 1940 spying mission to his 16 February 1942 diary entry: 'Right at the end of her stay he [Klop] discovered that she had Jewish blood and that Karl Drücke was also non-Aryan. This accounts for a great deal, particularly the attitude of ... [German intelligence] officers who refused to eat with them on their journey to Norway [en route for Scotland]. The whole expedition seems to have been extremely hurried and singularly ill-conceived. No details had been worked out and most parties concerned seemed to think the plan was doomed to failure ...'

6    Some sources say Vera was later interned on the Isle of Man, where many of the UK's 'enemy aliens' spent the war years.

7    It has been suggested that the name adopted in England by the woman who had so many pre-war aliases was Vera de Witt.

8    Mary Size later acquired near legendary status as the initial Governor of Askham Grange, Britain's first open prison for women, which opened in 1947. She pioneered a regime there that was noticeably more humane than anything that had gone before, treating prisoners with dignity and respect while giving them every opportunity to educate themselves. Miss Size remained at the Yorkshire prison until 1952.

# 12

# POTENT MIX: THE FORCES DRIVING DOROTHY

Filed at The National Archives in the midst of a raft of papers relating to the final six years of Dorothy O'Grady's imprisonment at Aylesbury lies a psychological report, dated 16 June 1944, in the scrawled handwriting of Dr Violet Minster, the prison's medical officer. There was very good reason for such an analysis. The opening sentence provides the first telling clue to the principal reasons behind Dorothy's life-long desire to create trouble for herself, to be noticed, to tell stories and mislead – and deliberately to risk her life in the process.

It reads, 'This patient has attacks, which she states occur at intervals, in which she has to "obey people" inside her who encourage her to do harmful acts to herself.'

These words serve as the prelude to a catalogue of deeply disturbing evidence about the true forces driving Dorothy. Much of the detail is shocking – in places, horrific. Abruptly, it jolts a hitherto rollicking spy story, admittedly dark in parts but generally underscored with lashings of mischievous light-heartedness, right out of its reverie and into a nightmarish new category altogether.

Finally, it joins up the dots to draw the undulating O'Grady legacy into its rightful place. A significantly enhanced element of sympathetic understanding emerges.

Dorothy had said, looking back on the events of 1940, that she 'must have been suffering from some sort of kink'. If the persona of Nazi spy had really been nothing more than misguided fantasy, it was palpably obvious that something was awry in her psychological make-up. Quite apart from the evidence of her earlier troubled history, who in their right mind would risk their life 'for a laugh'?

But, in all the many jaunts into her past, packed with detailed, often bizarre, revelations, when telling anyone who would listen about her extraordinary life story, Dorothy had never ventured far into the realms of the disturbed psychology that had brought her to the attention of an astonished world in 1940.

A fantasist and storyteller, a joker and thrill-seeker. She was happy to admit to all that. A child thrown off-kilter by the death of her beloved adoptive mother. A woman with a grudge, seeking a twisted sort of revenge on the British nation for a long-felt injustice. Yes, she was both of those things too. But the problem with Dorothy O'Grady was far more profound – and her only public concession to the existence of any deep-rooted psychological disturbance was that one, seemingly throwaway, phrase: 'I must have been suffering from some sort of kink'.

Dr Minster's report revealed that Dorothy's ill-balanced character as an adult was shaped at a very early stage of her life. 'She states that she was an adopted child,' wrote the MO:

> Her earliest recollections are of her adoptive mother reading the Bible to her after she had been playing about with her body while in her cot. Apparently, she has had these impulses all her life, before the onset of menstruation and ever since, and has been in the habit of putting things in her vagina.

Those words, while ambiguous without the detail that was to follow, were the first hint that the harmful self-inflicted acts Dr Minister had drawn attention to were some way distinct in nature from what might be termed common self-harm – and would prove to be of immense significance. The doctor's report continued, 'Although married at 28 years to a man of 48 years [Vincent was actually 47 at the time of the marriage and Dorothy, 29], she has had little sexual intercourse – always hurried to get it over so that her husband could go back to his own room.'

This sentence hinted at a marital relationship somewhat less perfect than that suggested by Vincent O'Grady in the wake of his wife's 1940 trial when he had spoken of the couple's 'fifteen years of happiness together ... she was a good wife'.

So was there a link between Dorothy's sexual impulses and her 'thrilling' flirtation with execution in the Second World War? According to Dr Minster, there was: 'She has told me that she regretted sometimes that the capital sentences were not carried out as she would have liked to experience it, and that she enjoyed her trial' – a statement which broadly mirrored Dorothy's own account.

But what followed in the next paragraphs of the medical officer's report was altogether new and profoundly disturbing. Unpleasant though much of the detail undoubtedly seems, it is essential to a proper understanding of Dorothy's extreme psycho-sexual imbalance. 'She says she has sometimes placed a chair on her bed so that she can pretend she is being executed,' wrote Dr Minster:

Sometimes she feels compelled to lie naked under her bed at night, and does in fact do so.

Her commonest compulsion is to insert foreign bodies into her vagina. I have removed a pot – a 6oz medicinal measure – and on another occasion, 50 pieces of broken glass (she stated there were 50 pieces inserted and the numbers were correct). These articles had been left in for 12 hours before she had reported the fact. These times, however, when I have had to remove the foreign bodies [were] only when she hadn't been able to remove them herself, but one night she inserted an electric light bulb which she removed herself next morning.

Dr Minster concluded that O'Grady was fit for transfer to 'an appropriate prison' for psychological investigation and treatment, adding – over optimistically as it turned out – that 'this patient is intelligent and should co-operate in treatment'. Dorothy's intellect would be the subject of the opening lines in a lengthy report compiled in September 1944 by Dr Jean Durrant – the psychotherapist Sidney Rodin later approached for his *Sunday Express* article in 1950 – after a reluctant Dorothy had been transferred back to Holloway jail for the investigation recommended by Dr Minster in June. The transfer had taken place the following month and evidently Dorothy had been seen several times by Dr Durrant prior to the issue of the psychotherapist's report on 6 September.

'Mrs O'Grady is a woman of very superior intelligence,' began Dr Durrant. 'On the Binet Scale she had an IQ of 140 and on Raven's matrices [used for testing non-verbal reasoning] her score was only one point off the highest class.' Evidently, whatever else she was, Dorothy O'Grady was very far from 'dotty'.[1]

'Had she had a good home background and education,' added Dr Durrant:

> her ability would probably have been directed into profitable channels, and her emotional development proceeded along normal lines. She was, however, illegitimate, and nothing is known of her parents. She was adopted and, on the death of the mother and remarriage of the father to his housekeeper, she and her education were neglected. On leaving school, she became a domestic servant and then a prostitute.

There was no mention here of a wrongful soliciting arrest.

'This upbringing may have caused, and has certainly increased, a deep feeling of resentment and hatred towards people in general, which has steadily developed since childhood. She states that she loves deceiving people "for a joke" and that the only real affection she feels is for animals.' The marriage to Vincent O'Grady was now sounding even less of a love match than it had appeared.

'Side by side with this resentment,' noted Jean Durrant at the start of what was very probably the most significant, and certainly the most poignant, few lines of her psychological appraisal:

176

there has grown up a strong masochistic tendency, which has recently become a compulsion. From her earliest years she remembers masturbating and discovering that the rough gloves which her parents tied on to prevent the habit only increased her pleasure in it. As she was a solitary child with few friends, she had ample opportunity for indulging the symptom, and remembers it was associated with a good deal of phantasy [sic].

The fantasy element, Dr Durrant continued, had become 'much more marked' since Dorothy's trial, 'and she imagines she is being tortured to make her confess'.

Further observations vital to the process of constructing a definitive profile of O'Grady followed from the psychotherapist: 'At no time, however, does she entertain definite delusions, and fear of discovery can always terminate the fantasy. She also indulges in other masochistic practices, such as tying herself up, and all her life she has enjoyed punishment, and has often sought it unnecessarily.'

Dr Durrant's patient also displayed 'some hysterical features', but the psychotherapist was not persuaded these were genuine: 'I am inclined to think some of these may be frank malingering in order to avoid doing what she dislikes.'

Perceptions of what is 'normal' in terms of female sexuality have, of course, changed substantially since the 1940s, but even to the eye of the twenty-first-century reader, it is obvious that there were plenty of genuinely disturbing aspects to Dorothy's complex personality for the doctor to mull over. 'In view of her age, and the nature and length of her symptoms, treatment, even with full co-operation, would necessarily be prolonged, and the prognosis is doubtful – and I do not think there is any likelihood of her being cured by psychotherapy here.'

Dr Durrant's reasons for this bleak assessment then followed:

In the first place she still derives a certain amount of sexual pleasure from her practices and only at times really wishes to rid herself of them. In the second, she so much dislikes Holloway, as compared with Aylesbury, that it is quite impossible for her to co-operate fully in a treatment which she knows to have been the cause of her transfer.

Apart from a fear of falling bombs, 'the other prisoners taunt her with being a spy, and the life here is so much more restricted that she becomes depressed and miserable, and unable to give her attention to psychological treatment – while the increased solitude gives her more time to indulge her symptoms.'

This insightful report from September 1944, in which so much of the defining truth about Dorothy O'Grady had lain hidden from public view for sixty-three years, concluded:

> Since the only period of her life in which she has refrained from masturbation and masochistic practices has been when her energies have been fully occupied in running a boarding house, I should recommend that she should return to Aylesbury and be given as much mental and physical occupation as is possible in prison, bearing in mind her superior intelligence and ability.

Dorothy was returned to Aylesbury the same month. On 26 September Jean Durrant approached the prison commissioners with a written request. Admitting that she had investigated her patient 'without much success', she added that O'Grady 'would like to write and tell me how her symptoms are getting on – if she can do so without her letters being seen before they leave Aylesbury'. Dr Durrant had 'no idea' whether or not this would help, but said she had promised her patient that she would write and seek the commissioners' permission.

There was another reason for the request. The psychotherapist added that she found O'Grady 'a very interesting case and should be glad to know how she progresses, if possible'. Dr Durrant seems to have struck up a rapport with Dorothy, who evidently had enthused to the doctor about her ability to pursue her love of tending the Aylesbury prison garden. Jean Durrant concluded her letter in light-hearted vein: 'She has told me so often how much she enjoys the life at

Aylesbury, and all about it, that I really feel I know it quite well. I hope the tomatoes of which she has spoken so much were not all perished before she got back!'

There is no record of how the Aylesbury tomatoes had fared. More seriously, there is no record either of whether or not the psychotherapist's request was granted.

However, it is clear from the prison records that, once back in the familiar, less restricted, environment of the Buckinghamshire jail, Dorothy was content to toe the line – though the concerns for her mental health had certainly not abated. On 28 March 1945 Aylesbury governor Mary Size told the prison commissioners that Dorothy had 'steadied down very well since the early years of her sentence', but she remained 'a very difficult psychological problem'.

Added the governor:

> I cannot be very hopeful about the future, but if she shows signs of being willing to co-operate with the psychotherapist I would propose to again transfer her to Holloway for consideration. It was thought at Holloway that her great fear of bombing had something to do with her lack of co-operation in the treatment.

By late March 1945 the threat of aerial attack on London by Germany had diminished dramatically following the capture in France by the Allied armies of the launch sites for the V-1 'Doddlebug' flying bombs. Mary Size clearly hoped that this would have a positive impact on O'Grady.[2]

However, while the possibility of returning Dorothy to Holloway for treatment was several times discussed in 1945, it never happened, although, on 21 June 1945, she was again the subject of a formal report from Dr Durrant at Holloway. Much of what the psychotherapist wrote reiterated the substance of her earlier report, but there were several new details. among them confirmation from Dorothy that she had not seen, or heard of, her adoptive father, George Squire, since she entered domestic service following her period of training in London.

There was also the psychotherapist's apparent unquestioning acceptance that Dorothy in the summer of 1940 had 'pursued activities which she herself states were all a hoax because it amused her to make people think she was a spy'.

The report elaborated further on Dorothy's sexual compulsions: 'Ever since she can remember, she has masturbated a great deal, and at the age of five she recalls that she found it more stimulating if she wore a rough glove and hurt herself in the process. As time has gone by, the masochistic element has become steadily stronger.' This had led to the bodily insertions, 'till recently' of 'large and painful objects' (an example used in the report to highlight the horrific nature of this was that of 100 pins) and her practice of tying herself up 'in uncomfortable positions for hours on end'. Added Dr Durrant, 'She says she was never really interested in heterosexual intercourse, and only did it for money.'

Jean Durrant then commented on Dorothy's condition on examination: 'Physically she was healthy and showed no signs of psychosis.' As the doctor would tell Sidney Rodin in 1950, Dorothy could not, therefore, be classed as insane.

With regard to her patient's progress since examination in the summer of 1944, the psychotherapist could say only that:

> ... as she very much disliked being transferred from Aylesbury, and it was in any case the time of the flying bombs, she was never at any time wholly co-operative, and though she said she wished to be cured, I do not think she did so wholeheartedly, as her practices obviously afforded her a good deal of enjoyment as well as discomfort.

Dr Durrant reiterated that Dorothy's age (46) and the length of the period she had exhibited her various symptoms were also 'contra-indications to treatment'. She added, 'It was thought very unlikely that at this stage psychotherapy would remove either her masochism or the very strong sense of resentment against society fostered by her upbringing and environment. Treatment was therefore not considered.'

In Dr Durrant's opinion, expressed in a succinct diagnosis, Dorothy was a 'hysterical psychopath' – destined to remain that way for the foreseeable future.

This is a highly complex field. Put simply, Dorothy was displaying some features of an hysterical personality interspersed with the sort of psychopathic (or anti-social personality disorder) tendencies that often produce addictive problems.[3]

It is perhaps sadly ironic that the list of prominent individuals who have been described as hysterical psychopaths includes Adolf Hitler. This is a far better indication of how widely the term has been applied than it is of any real likeness between Mrs Dorothy O'Grady and the man she once purported to serve.

The remainder of her prison term is something of a microcosm of her turbulent life. She had long since dropped her once proudly borne persona of a convicted wartime Nazi spy when Aylesbury's prison governor Mary Size reported favourably to the prison commissioners on 21 September 1945 that O'Grady had 'behaved well recently. She gets on peacefully with the other "special stage" women and is no trouble at present.' The governor explained that Dorothy 'is employed on repairs (needlework) which she does exceptionally well, and though she likes to have notice taken of her and sometimes fusses over trivial details, I consider that she is adapting herself satisfactorily to life here at the present time'.[4]

According to a medical report the same month, Dorothy's health was 'very good'. She had gained 14lb since admission to Aylesbury in 1941. While 'still introspective', she had made no more attempts to hurt herself by bodily insertions. So long as notice was taken of her, 'all her complaints are minor ones'.

The situation was nothing like as rosy in October. A report from the jail's medical officer at the start of the month revealed that Dorothy had 'given a lot of trouble'. It had nothing to do with a mild attack of rheumatism in her leg – there was still nothing seriously wrong with her health – but she had been what the MO called 'very hysterical' and had caused 'a lot of trouble with the other "special stage" women in D Hall.

Unless she is separated from these women, five of whom are of similar highly strung temperament – three Irish, one Russian and one German – I am afraid physical violence may occur between them.'

Governor Size contributed by adding that Dorothy had:

> ... deteriorated rapidly in the last few days and was reported yesterday for causing a disturbance and using abusive language. I remanded her for one week to give her chance to pull herself together. This morning, however, there was a further disturbance which has greatly upset the other women in D Hall. I therefore suggest that O'Grady be removed to another prison as she is unfit for the privileges of this establishment.

There was agreement at Aylesbury that the change of scenery at Holloway – despite Dorothy's dogged reluctance to go there – had done her good and, if Dr Durrant could take her on again, another break from Aylesbury's routine might also prove beneficial as she still had a significant period of her sentence to serve.

The joint report was sent to the prison commissioners, who quickly authorised transfer to Holloway for the 'further assistance of Dr Durrant'. The transfer followed on 19 October. It was a disaster. Jean Durrant found Dorothy 'quite unsuitable for psychotherapy ...'. On 2 February 1946 Holloway moved to evict her.

The prison's governor said they 'would be grateful if Dorothy O'Grady could be transferred to Aylesbury'. They were finding it difficult to deal with her. She was 'antagonising the other women in the wing'. The governor added, 'Dr Durrant informs me that she is unable to do anything for her as O'Grady will not co-operate.' Duly dispatched, Dorothy headed for Buckinghamshire once more.

And there she stayed. It seems fair to assume that prison staff at both Aylesbury and Holloway would at that point have been relieved to see the back of O'Grady for good. But, early in 1946, on paper at least, she still had another nine years of her fourteen-year sentence to serve. How much Vincent O'Grady knew of his wife's travails – or, indeed, of the outcome of her psychological examination – remains a matter for conjecture, but in March 1946 he was doing his utmost to bring her incarceration at the nation's expense to a premature close, eliciting the help of anyone he could think of, MPs included, to get her out.

His protestations that prison was having a bad effect on her health fell on deaf ears. He was reminded that she had undergone a successful hysterectomy that had improved her physical condition, had suffered no further serious physical health problems and, while she had not been treated for her psychological imbalance, this was entirely down to her. The situation was summarised by medical officer Violet Minster: 'Prison is not having any adverse effects on her health.'

In the end, her personal requests to the Home Secretary for an early release, aided by her husband's own failing health and her appeals to be able to look after him, produced the desired result. She would serve only nine years. But as her release date in February 1950 drew near, the prison authorities at Aylesbury could muster only the gloomiest of forecasts for her future prospects when freed.

The governor reported on 19 November 1949 that 'the outlook for this woman is not hopeful, as long imprisonment has increased her egotism and she will have little support from her husband. She must however at least try to resume her married life with the help of close [post-release] supervision ...'. If that wasn't bleak enough, the contribution from the medical staff most certainly was: 'I think this woman will remain what she has always been – a cunning woman with a nasty, bitter streak in her which no form of psychotherapy will eradicate. Physical senility may make her less troublesome, but I doubt it very much.'

This unsympathetic assessment came from Violet Minster's successor as the prison's medical officer, a Dr Matthews, who clearly had failed to develop anything remotely resembling the kind of understanding and concern demonstrated by both Dr Minster and Holloway's psychotherapist, Jean Durrant.

Dorothy O'Grady would not have been aware of these disparaging remarks. Had she been told, it is probable that she would have taken very little notice. Her mind was elsewhere as her final Christmas in prison approached. She had written her autobiography and now she needed the permission of the prison authorities to take it with her when she was discharged. Alerted to this in December 1949, the prison commissioners were told by Aylesbury's governor, 'I feel this was written more than nine years ago and that O'Grady brought it on transfer.'

The matter had yet to be resolved two months later when, on 22 February 1950, just two days before Dorothy's release, the prison commissioners were still agonising over the fate of her 'short autobiography'. Should the request to take it with her be approved? Perhaps the document could be sent to O'Grady *after* her discharge? In truth, there was as much deliberation over the circumstances under which O'Grady was allowed the paper and the elastic band, in which her story was secured. The commissioners and the prison's governor suspected that Dorothy wanted to use her autobiography as the draft for a press story. Eventually, there was agreement among all concerned that the request should be disallowed.

Some months later, with Dorothy long gone from Aylesbury, the prison governor noted that 'the autobiography is provisionally being retained'. Dorothy's story would instead be placed within the files making up her prison record.

It isn't there today. But that, as events transpired, is academic. Dorothy knew her story off by heart; it was very well rehearsed in her mind. She didn't really need the prompt of a written account when she hot-footed it to the *Sunday Express*.

There can no longer be any doubt that what she told Sidney Rodin and so many others in the years that followed was, by and large, the truth. She had never been a Nazi agent. But it wasn't the whole truth. She hadn't just pretended to be one for a giggle. Her wartime infamy was not just the huge joke at the nation's expense she always claimed it had been. It was the result of a potent mix of psycho-sexual complexities, dating right back to her childhood, that, one day in August 1940, compelled her to adopt the colourful persona of the spy beside the sea.

# Notes

1   Raven's Matrices measure reasoning powers by means of non-verbal multiple choice solutions to puzzles. They were originally developed by John C. Raven in 1936. In each test, the subject is asked to identify the missing element that completes a pattern.

2   Attacks by the V-1 flying bombs ceased altogether on 29 March 1945, the day after Mary Size's report for the prison commissioners on Dorothy O'Grady, when the last operating launch site was overrun.

3   See 'The differentiation of hysterical personality from hysterical psychopathy', an article by A.D. Forrest, first published in the *British Journal of Medical Psychology*, volume 40, issue 1 (1967), now available online.

4   Special stage prisoners (referred to by O'Grady as 'special prisoners') were those granted certain privileges on reaching an advanced stage of imprisonment.

# BIBLIOGRAPHY

Anon., 'State Secrets – The Unmasking of Klop, Secret Agent',
  Hideaway Publications Ltd. website (2010).

Anon., 'The Village – The German Spies', portgordon.org (2010).

Benois, Nadia and Ustinov, Peter, *Klop and the Ustinov Family* (London:
  Sidgwick & Jackson, 1973).

Bray, Peter and Brown, Fay, *The Ventnor Area at War 1939–1945* (Isle of
  Wight: Ventnor Local History Society, 1989).

Cantwell, Anthony and Sprack, Peter, *The Needles Defences* (Isle of Wight:
  The Redoubt Consultancy, 1986).

Coldham, Phil, 'The Beautiful Spy', veraschalburgg.com (2010).

Dean, Mike, *Radar on the Isle of Wight* (Lincoln: Historical Radar Society,
  1994).

Forrest, A.D., 'The Differentiation of Hysterical Personality from
  Hysterical Psychopathy', *British Journal of Medical Psychology* (1967).

Friel, James, *Careless Talk* (London: Macmillan, 1992).

Hayward, James, *Myths & Legends of the Second World War* (Stroud: Sutton
  Publishing, 2003).

Hill, Peter, 'The Spy Who Never Was', *British Journalism Review* (1995).

Hinsley, Sir F.H. (ed.), *British Intelligence in the Second World War* (Cambridge:
  Cambridge University Press, 1993).

*Keesing's Contemporary Archive of World Events* (London: Keesing's Ltd.,
  1940).

Kluiters, F.A.C. and Verhoeyen, E., 'An International Spymaster and Mystery Man: Abwehr Officer Hilmar G. J. Dierks and his Agents', Kluiters & Verhoeyen website (undated).

Masterman, J.C., *The Double Cross System in the War of 1939 to 1945* (USA: Yale University Press, 1972).

Merrilees, Gary, 'Wee Willie Merrilees: Scotland's Most Famous Policeman', Merrilees Family Association website, *Reader's Digest* (London: 1960).

Merrilees, William, *The Short Arm of the Law: The Memoirs of William Merrilees OBE* (London: John Long, 1966).

Mitchell, Garry with Cantwell, Anthony, Cobb, Peter and Sprack, Peter, *Spit Bank and the Spithead Forts* (Kent: G.H. Mitchell, 1988).

Murphy, Sean, *Letting the Side Down: British Traitors of the Second World War* (Stroud: The History Press, 2003).

Peters, Kevin, 'DORA, U35 and the Cat: A Story of Spies and Aylesbury Prison', *Aylesbury Town Matters* (Aylesbury Town Council, 2010).

Ramsey, Winston G. (ed.), 'German Spies in Britain: The Unlucky Sixteen', *After the Battle* (London: Battle of Britain Prints International Ltd., 1976).

Rowe, Mark, *Don't Panic: Britain Prepares for Invasion, 1940* (Stroud: The History Press, 2010).

Reid, Peter H., *Port Gordon: The Life and Times of a Village* (Moray: Tynet Heritage, 1997).

Searle, Adrian, *The Isle of Wight at War 1939–45* (Wimborne: The Dovecote Press, 1989).

West, Nigel (ed.), *The Guy Liddell Diaries, vol. 1: 1939–42* (Abingdon: Routledge, 2009).

Zimmerman, David, *Britain's Shield: Radar and the Defeat of the Luftwaffe* (Stroud: Amberley Publishing, 2010).

## Principal Original Sources

The National Archives, Kew, London: HO 45/25408 – Dorothy O'Grady prosecution and trial, 1940. PCOM 9/1497 – Dorothy O'Grady prison records 1918–50. HO 144/21636 – Karl Drücke and

Werner Walti (Robert Petter) prosecution, trial and execution, 1940–41. KV 2/107 – Jose Waldburgh capture and trial. KV 2/12 – Carl Meiger capture and trial. KV 2/11 Charles can den Kierboom capture and trial. ADM/188/323 – Vincent O'Grady naval service record. ADM/139/688 – Joseph O'Grady naval service record.

The National Archives (online): censuses for England and Wales, 1881 – Vincent O'Grady residence, Sutton, Surrey; 1891 – Vincent O'Grady residence, Sutton, Surrey; 1901 – Dorothy Squire residence, Clapham, London. Vincent O'Grady residence, Gillingham, Kent; 1911 – Dorothy Squire residence, Paddington, London. Vincent O'Grady residence, Whitechapel, London.

Registration District, Holborn, London – Vincent O'Grady birth certificate, 1879.

Registration District, Maldon, Essex – Vincent O'Grady and Dorothy Squire wedding certificate, 1926.

Registration District, Isle of Wight – Vincent O'Grady death certificate, 1953. Dorothy O'Grady death certificate, 1985.

Isle of Wight County Records Office, Newport: Electoral rolls 1933–80 – Vincent and Dorothy O'Grady residence. ARP records, 1939–45.

Isle of Wight County Library Service (local collection), Somerton: Holiday guides, Sandown and Shanklin 1936–49 – Vincent and Dorothy O'Grady residence. Isle of Wight street directories (Kelly's) 1931–51 – Vincent and Dorothy O'Grady residence.

Essex County Records Office, Chelmsford: electoral rolls 1926 – Dorothy Squire residence.

British Library (Newspaper Library), Colindale, London: newspapers and periodicals (various dates 1940–2000), UK – *Daily Express*, *Daily Herald*, *Daily Mail*, *Daily Mirror*, *Daily Telegraph*, *Isle of Wight Chronicle*, *Isle of Wight County Press*, *Isle of Wight Guardian*, *Isle of Wight Times*, *Isle of Wight Weekly Post*, *Reveille*, *Southern Evening Echo* (Southampton), *Sunday Express*, *Sunday Times*, *The Independent*, *The News* (Portsmouth), *The Times*, *Today*. Australia – *The Argus* (Melbourne). New Zealand – *Evening Post* (Wellington).

# INDEX

*Isle of Wight Weekly Post*
  45–6, 95, 98–9
Italy 21–2, 35–6

Jakobs, Josef 20
Jeffreys, Judge George 59,
  64–5
Job, Oswald 22
Joyce, William (Lord
  Haw-Haw) 20, 141

Kell, Vernon 17, 26–7
Kent 61
  Chatham 89–90
  Folkestone 33
  Gillingham 89
  Maidstone, HMP 132
  Ramsgate 31–2, 38
Kent, Tyler 142
Key, Jose 22
Kluiters, F.A.C. &
  Verhoeyen, E. 147–9,
  159
Kieboom, Charles van den
  61, 65, 110

Lahousen, Erwin von 150,
  156, 160
Liddell, Guy 124–5, 158,
  164–6, 171
Lipman, Maureen 101
Lisle, Alice 57, 65
Lloyd George, David 18
London 40, 48, 63–4, 74–5,
  80, 93, 107, 118, 135,
  142, 148–51, 156, 160,
  167, 179
  Bethnal Green 90
  Blitz, the 48
  Chelsea 131
  Clapham (& Convent
    of Notre Dame) 105,
    129–31, 142
  fire brigade 41, 63, 65,
    90, 102
  East Ham 89
  Edgware 131
  Harrow 105, 130

Holborn 89, 101
Holloway, HMP 50, 61,
  64, 80, 83, 87, 110,
  117–18, 130, 132, 135,
  137–41, 158, 176–9,
  182–3
Latchmere (Camp 020)
  24, 27
London Female
  Preventative &
  Reformatory
  Institution 131–3
Metropolitan Police 102,
  156
Old Bailey 18, 20, 65,
  67–8, 82, 132, 141,
  157
Pentonville, HMP 20–2,
  65, 110
Soho 119, 122
Tower of London 18, 21
Wandsworth, HMP 20–2,
  73, 157
London & North Eastern
  Railway 152
Lyme Regis, Dorset 32

Macnaghten, Malcolm 56,
  59, 65, 81
Major, John 103
Masterman, J.C. 24, 27
McAlister, Bob 45–6, 51
Mead, Albion & Maria 136
Meier, Carl 65, 110
Merrilees, William 156, 160
*Melbourne Argus*, Aus. 70
Merritt, Mike 104–5, 108,
  113, 115–16, 118–19
Minster, Violet 173–7, 183
MI5 (Security Service) 12,
  17, 23–5, 27, 37, 54,
  80, 98, 110, 117, 121,
  124, 139, 141, 145–7,
  149, 157–60, 162–3,
  165, 167
Mola, Emilio 25–6
Molotov, Vyacheslav 27
Murphy, Rose 111, 122

Napoleonic Wars
  (1799–1815) 18
The National Archives
  (Public Record Office)
  13, 15, 24, 74, 104,
  125–8, 164, 173
National Fire Service 50
Northampton 129
Norway 172
  Stavanger 151–2

O'Grady, Dorothy
  alias (Pamela Arland) 80,
    106–7, 130, 132, 134
  birth & early life 16, 62,
    76, 98–100, 105, 117,
    128–32, 142, 176–7
  court proceedings 11,
    49–50, 52–4, 60, 65–8,
    71, 80–2, 107–8,
    129–31, 137
  criminal record 13, 106,
    118, 130, 133–5
  death 12, 100
  imprisonment 15–16,
    71, 74–5, 81, 97–9,
    110–11, 118–19,
    132–3, 137–43,
    161–71, 173–85
  links with German spies
    / sympathisers 16, 23,
    140, 158–9, 162–7
  military arrest 9–11, 42,
    44–6, 76–7, 79
  police arrest 48–9, 51,
    80, 111–12, 120
  perceptions of 9, 11–16,
    25–6, 37–8, 40–2,
    47, 52, 54, 57, 62
    70–2, 74–5, 77, 83–5,
    92–4, 97, 100, 104–6,
    110, 112–18, 121,
    124, 131–4, 136,
    141, 161–3, 167–71,
    173–84
O'Grady, Agnes 75, 86,
  88, 91
O'Grady, Hannah 89